THE LIGHT AND THE DARK

THE LIGHT AND THE DARK

(THE LIFE AND TIMES OF ARTEMISIA GENTILESCHI)

A PLAY BY KATE HAMILL

With an introduction by Kristin Leahey

NORTHWESTERN UNIVERSITY PRESS

EVANSTON, ILLINOIS

Northwestern University Press
www.nupress.northwestern.edu

Printed in the United States of America

10 9 8 7 6 5 4 3 2 1

ISBN 979-8-89948-111-6 (paper)
ISBN 979-8-89948-112-3 (ebook)

Cataloging-in-Publication Data are available from the Library of Congress.

This play is for survivors.

CONTENTS

Introduction by Kristin Leahey ix

Production History xviii

The Light and the Dark 1

INTRODUCTION

Kristin Leahey

When encountering the work of the Italian Baroque painter Orazio Gentileschi (1563–1639) in museums, it is common to see him described on the object label as a Tuscan painter and a contemporary of the renowned Caravaggio. You will see no mention of the subjects he gravitated toward (as many were common to the period—religious iconography, mythological scenes, and portraits) or his biography. But when you experience the work of his daughter, Artemisia Gentileschi, descriptions always merge her art, its subjects, and her personal history as a young woman.

For instance, at the Getty Center in Los Angeles, which displays paintings by both father and daughter, on the placard for Artemisia Gentileschi's 1627 *Lucretia*, Lucretia is described as a heroic figure who was raped by the son of the king of Rome and who publicly called for vengeance before she took her own life, refusing to live as an "unchaste" woman. The label goes on to describe how the subject likely resonated with the artist, since Artemisia "experienced sexual violence as a young woman."[1] At the age of eighteen, Artemisia was raped by a fellow artist and friend of her father's—Agostino Tassi. When it was discovered, a famous trial, mostly concerning the theft of several of her and her father's paintings by Tassi, ensued in the haphazard Italian courts, wherein Artemisia was physically tortured to confess regarding the rape. Although the family won the case, the public did not consider her a chaste woman but at fault. In the art world, she subsequently was often portrayed as oppressed and victimized rather than defiant and subversive.

Another gallery label at the Getty, titled "Artemisia Gentileschi and the Female Hero," describes how the artist often depicted donne forti (strong women) and states that she "approached her subjects with great empathy and translated their experiences into emotionally complex and technically accomplished paintings."[2] Her legacy as an artist is not only about her being one of the most renowned female painters of the Baroque era but about how she was assaulted and then chastised and sexualized by society for her victimization. Artemisia Gentileschi, like many women lauded for their artistic work, can never be known simply as an artist who painted strong iconic women and self-portraits. Despite there being numerous films, TV shows, and plays rendering reliable or, often, fallacious variations of her life story, her work or the little that is attributed to her is not shown as widely as her father's, who often took credit for her paintings.

Unsurprisingly, Artemisia was and is considered the far better artist. The authorship of her work has been in debate since its inception and continues today. Both in subject and in form, Artemisia was creating something that had not been done before: bringing more light into the paintings and juxtaposing the strong, central women of her artwork with other women and with men, with female subjects often surpassing the power of the male figures. Men, whether they were the central subject in the Renaissance and Baroque painting or not, were always the primary focus. The Baroque period (the seventeenth and the first half of the eighteenth century) is characterized by ornateness, lavish design, and elaborate architecture, which originated in Italy and then flourished throughout Europe. Artemisia was also surpassing her male colleagues in terms of technique. Her work is found throughout the world and in galleries and museums such as the Getty in Los Angeles; the Metropolitan Museum of Art in New York; the Kimball Art Museum in Fort Worth, Texas; the Wadsworth Atheneum Museum of Art in Hartford, Connecticut; the Museum of Fine Arts in Budapest; the National Gallery in London; the Museo di Capodimonte in Naples; and the Uffizi Gallery in Florence.

Visting Florence, playwright Kate Hamill experienced Artemisia Gentileschi's 1620 interpretation of *Judith Beheading Holofernes*—her most famous painting and what has now become an invitation for women around the world to fight the patriarchy. Hamill, who is known as a feminist adaptor of literature into plays, decided to interpret not only a historic narrative but the lineage of a painting. *Judith Beheading Holofernes* was a popular Renaissance subject, frequently represented by Artemisia's male mentors and contemporaries, in which the Jewish widow Judith, traditionally depicted as either the seductresses or the ingenue in contemporaries' work, and her often seemingly malevolent and aged maidservant Abra were painted as the decapitators of the Assyrian general. Despite this act leading to the liberation of their city of Bethulia, the women often were rendered as criminals or victims by other artists who painted them in the seventeenth century or before. In her lifetime, Artemisia returned to the subject of *Judith* at least four to six times, beginning in 1612. She wrote a different narrative, making the women equals, working in tandem to save the city. Holofernes is marginalized in how he is positioned in the painting. Artemisia's *Judith Beheading Holofernes* became an icon for the contemporary feminist movement and for International Women's Day on March 8. For women like Hamill and myself, as her dramaturg, who are of a generation that is part of the #MeToo movement, it's a call to action.

Particularly in 2017, the #MeToo movement raised awareness of sexual harassment and assault against Women+, often at work but also in domestic environments, and bolstered survivors to share their experiences. Much of the movement began on social media and was rooted in the arts and entertainment industries, but women from every discipline could cite personal experiences or those of friends, colleagues, and family members. Artemisia was one of the first women, but certainly not the only one of her historical period or earlier, to share her experience of assault. In *Artemisia Gentileschi and Feminism in Early Modern Europe,* the biographer and scholar Mary D. Garrard writes that women were the legal property of their father or husband when the most famous female painter of the Baroque period was born in 1593.[3] The daughter of painter Orazio Gentileschi and Prudentia Montone was a child in Rome. When she turned twelve, Artemisia endured the loss of her mother, who died giving birth to Artemisia's youngest brother. Her family was artisanal working class, and her urban surroundings were rather violent though bohemian. She began her apprenticeship as a painter when she was fourteen years old, under the tutelage of her father.[4]

As a young adult, Artemisia was often isolated in her home, and only allowed to visit churches, where she would experience prominent art of the day. Besides having her father's somewhat watchful eye, she was poorly chaperoned by the family's tenant and occasional maid Donna Tuzia. In 1610, Agostino Tassi, a friend and fellow artist of her father's, began teaching Artemisia about perspective but also developed an obsession with the young woman; with little supervision, he would walk his pupil home from the studio.[5] The tête-à-tête resulted in one of the most infamous early Italian judicial cases of theft and assault. The rape of the child occurred at the family's home, in her father's bed; and she attempted to stab him with a knife from her father's bedside table. Artemisia later reported this and the testimony was recorded in the court documents. Tassi forced Artemisia to continue to have sex with him and to keep the assaults silent. He falsely promised marriage, despite being already married. He didn't disclose this to her, although it was well known in his circle of friends and colleagues. If it was discovered that Artemisia had sex with Tassi, it would further financially ruin her family.

The Protestant Church of England and the Roman Catholic Church both strongly enforced female virginity before marriage (a holdover from the medieval period and before). Virginity or maidenhood was a bargaining tool for women and their families and, for many, of any class, their only real asset; as a maiden, they also had the power to rise in society. Chastity fulfilled the perception that property was inherited by the rightful heirs. If virginity was lost outside of marriage, a woman lost her wealth by being disinherited and was shunned by the church and society in the medieval period (fifth to sixteenth centuries), the Renaissance (fourteenth to seventeenth centuries), and the Tudor period (1485 to 1603), and long after these historical epochs. Blame inevitably would be placed on the "unchaste" Artemisia, as it was on many women. As Jane Tibbetts Schulenburg writes in "The Heroics of Virginity: Brides of Christ and Sacrificial Mutilation," according to the Church the only way women could transcend their "unfortunate sexuality" was through "sexless perfection."[6] Men were not held to the same standards, especially those of the artisan class. For instance, Caravaggio, who was considered a master artist of the Baroque period, led a violent, libertine life, which was often glamorized. Artemisia was not afforded the same liberty. Her incredible paintings, which primarily depict female saints and strong historical women; this event; and the trial that followed simultaneously live on in infamy, as well as reverence.

As an artist, Artemisia was influenced not by the few female artists of the period, such as the prodigious Lavinia Fontana, who also lived in Rome, depicted the first female nude,[7] and was of immense esteem, but by male artists, such as Caravaggio and Michelangelo. Later, as a resident of Florence, she observed that circumstances for female artists were better there. She wanted to be assessed as male artists were, but she always felt the inequity throughout her lifetime and commented on the discrepancy through her work. To help overcome the stigma from the assault, she did marry. With her husband, Pierantonio Stiattesi (an apothecary, occasional artist, and her inconsistent business partner), she moved to Florence, and they had five children—only one (Prudentia) survived past the age of five.[8] Because of her husband's debts, she was often in litigation.

In October 1614, Artemisia attained patronage from the house of Medici when she was commissioned by Grand Duchess Maria Maddalena, a rare female patron, for three paintings, including the lost painting noted in the Medici inventory *Diana and the Eight Nymphs.*[9] In 1616, after a yearlong application process, she entered the highly selective Accademia delle Arti del Disegno, becoming its first woman painter. Gianfrancesco Loredan and Pietro Michiele were related to this group through their literary activities and worked with her. In 1618, she gained autonomy over her dowry, as well as her debts.[10] And she subsequently disengaged from her husband. She was likely involved with the young nobleman Francesco Maringhi.

In 1620, she left the Florentine court after the painting of *St. Mary Magdalen* (currently in the Uffizi). She also worked for the grand duke in Florence in a small group of artists. The Duke of Alcalá, specifically Fernando Enríquez Afán de Ribera, the third Duke, was her patron.[11] He purchased *St. Mary Magdalen* while serving as the Spanish ambassador in Rome in 1626. He later displayed the painting in his home in Seville. He shared Artemisia's interest in creativity, and we don't know if he simply gravitated toward the work as examples of female beauty or if there were investments of greater note, as Garrard notes in her text *Artemisia Gentileschi around 1622: The Shaping and Reshaping of an Artistic Identity*.[12] This notion of feminine beauty arises in female artists' self-portraiture and was common with many of Artemisia's patrons. The term "double beauty" means that the artist's appearance or beauty in the self-portrait is assumed to be her appearance in life, whether they were aesthetically pleasing or not.[13] In the Renaissance period and subsequently, this concept fueled male patrons buying self-portraits by female artists. Not only was the patron buying the portrait, but he thought he was buying a likeness of the artist or ostensibly the artist. Especially in Artemisia's case, patrons didn't separate her from her art. The resemblance of the actual Artemisia to the work is unknown.

By 1624, Artemisia and her daughter were back in Rome without her husband. She had a second daughter, likely by another father.[14] Both her daughters were trained to be painters, taught by their mother. In the 1630s, the successful painter lived in Venice (she begins to add background landscapes to her paintings, as her father eventually did as well), then Naples, and by 1640 England. In the 1640s, she eventually returned to Naples, still actively working and being commissioned. And the proto-feminist painter of women of history, heroism, and the most defiant and relentless *Judith Slaying Holofernes* died in 1656 at the age of sixty.

Garrard writes, "In Artemisia's fantasized inversion of gender stereotype, Judith is a socially liberated woman who punishes masculine wrongdoing. Although none of Artemisia's Judiths is literally a self-portrait, the artist seems to have embedded coded self-references in each of her versions of the theme."[15] Sixty paintings are attributed to her, but some of her work has been lost and some still possibly inaccurately credited to her father. Artemisia as an artist needed a savvy business sense. She said to her patron Don Antonio Ruffo, "A woman's name raises doubts until her work is seen."[16] The rape trial did bring her attention, but infamy and grappling with her public image made it difficult for her to sell her work. She was a female artist engaging with a society that was as preoccupied with Baroque art as it was with popular culture and the artists' lives, especially if they could be sensationalized.

Artemisia was in constant need of finding patrons. She was sending unsolicited paintings to potential future male patrons of the aristocracy, such as Francesco I d'Este, Duke of Moderna, and Ferdinando II de' Medici in Florence.[17] Her life was never easy. Artemisia's experiences clearly influenced her presentation of visual narratives with dominant female and subordinate male figures, highlighting a distinctive proto-feminist artistic voice. The women she paints are robust and not petite or genteel in shape. The heroines in her paintings are not depictions of victimization or violence or revenge or hate but rather she's providing them voice, agency, and social equity—whereas servants come across as the same stature as nobility or an artist of the artisan class. Her paintings of self-portraiture appear as strong as a mythical queen. Garrard contends, "In her early years especially, one sees her trying on personae like hats, playing . . . a suffering Susanna, an argumentative Lucretia, a commanding Cleopatra, a vile Judith, a queenly Ester."[18] But despite the breadth, the nuance, and the brilliance of her work, she struggled to overcome her victimization, which is clear by the financial struggles as well. Garrard opines that the artist enlarged the notion of beauty to include women who protested rape and killed men, in a society that accepted rape and/or murder of women as commonplace.[19] Art and literature embraced and naturalized assault.

Artemisia's work speaks not only for herself but represents many women of the past and the present. Her identity was formed and reformed by her public personae, her work, and her subversive references. The art possesses an abundance of hermeneutic interpretations that evolve over centuries. This was the case for Hamill, who witnessed the mistreatment, sometimes in the form of harassment and sometimes to the degree of misconduct and assault, of female colleagues and friends in the theater industry. This in part, like many female artists including Artemisia, propelled a strong feminist streak in her work. Hamill has the facility to label her work feminist. The subversive and progressive Artemisia did not. Lacking the historical precedent of the word "feminist," we can comfortably label her a proto-feminist. As Garrard argues, "If her art makes us think and talk about sexual violence, stereotypical femininity, the beauty myth, and most of all, about feminism, it must be conceded that she has given the early twenty-first century a seismological blueprint for a discussion that is, unfortunately, still relevant and meaningful."[20] As one in four women have experienced sexual assault and most rapes remain unreported, the precedent for the work continues. The effects of assault remain the same and perhaps have even grown, such as risk for sexually transmitted diseases, post-traumatic stress disorder, the loss of employment and friends and family, and dependencies on drugs and alcohol. But many women, like Artemisia, fight and use their talents as a tool to survive. Hamill was adamant to tell the story of the artist and not the court case and not one of a victim but rather a survivor. We live in a society where the oppression and silence of women persists, perpetrated by men at every level of stature and office. The power and relevance of Artemisia's work continues to grow, as does its reach and impact, which changed the art world and gave hope for future generations of women.

NOTES

I would like to profoundly thank Megan Stielstra, Anne Gendler, Faith Wilson Stein, and Northwestern University Press for their keen editorial eyes, immense dedication, and incredible efforts toward the publication of this work. I would also like to acknowledge the tremendous labor of Katy Zapanta from the Michael Moore Agency, as well as that of Beth Blickers. Thank you to Boston University School of Theatre for support of this publication and its playwright. Kate Hamill and I have much gratitude for all the artists and organizations that have worked on the theatrical production of this work, in particular Primary Stages and Chautauqua Theater Company. And I would like to thank Kate Hamill for her incredible play, having me on the journey, and the beauty through the challenge Kate captures with this important work of art.

1. Gentileschi, Artemesia. General Collection. *Lucretia*. Los Angeles: Getty Museum, 2023.
2. Gentileschi, Artemesia. General Collection. Los Angeles: Getty Museum, 2023.
3. Mary D. Garrard, *Artemisia Gentileschi and Feminism in Early Modern Europe* (Reaktion Books, 2023), 13.
4. Garrard, *Artemisia Gentileschi and Feminism in Early Modern Europe*, 22.
5. Garrard, *Artemisia Gentileschi and Feminism in Early Modern Europe*, 23.
6. Jane Tibbetts Schulenburg, "The Heroics of Virginity: Brides of Christ and Sacrificial Mutilation," in *Women in the Middle Ages and the Renaissance: Literary and Historical Perspectives*, ed. Mary Beth Rose (Syracuse University Press, 1986), 31.
7. In 1613, Fontana painted *Minerva Dressing*, which is in Rome's Galleria Borghese. It is the first painting by a female artist to depict nudes.
8. Garrard, *Artemisia Gentileschi and Feminism in Early Modern Europe*, 26–27.
9. Garrard, *Artemisia Gentileschi and Feminism in Early Modern Europe*, 28.
10. Garrard, *Artemisia Gentileschi and Feminism in Early Modern Europe*, 32.
11. Garrard, *Artemisia Gentileschi and Feminism in Early Modern Europe*, 36.
12. Mary D. Garrard, *Artemisia Gentileschi around 1622: The Shaping and Reshaping of an Artistic Identity* (University of California Press, 2001), 72.
13. Garrard, *Artemisia Gentileschi around 1622*, 7.
14. Garrard, *Artemisia Gentileschi and Feminism in Early Modern Europe*, 35.
15. Garrard, *Artemisia Gentileschi around 1622*, 19-20.
16. Garrard, *Artemisia Gentileschi around 1622*, 106.
17. Garrard, *Artemisia Gentileschi around 1622*, 106.
18. Garrard, *Artemisia Gentileschi around 1622*, 22.
19. Garrard, *Artemisia Gentileschi around 1622*, 15.
20. Garrard, *Artemisia Gentileschi around 1622*, 123.

PRODUCTION HISTORY

The world premiere of *The Light and the Dark (The Life and Times of Artemisia Gentileschi)* was August 15, 2024, at Chautauqua, New York. It was coproduced by Chautauqua Theater Company (Jade King Carroll, producing artistic director; Emily Glinick, general manager) and Primary Stages.

The Light and the Dark then received its New York Off-Broadway premiere in November 2024 at 59E59 Theatres in New York City, in a production by Primary Stages (with Erin Daley, artistic director; Shane D. Hudson, executive director; Casey Childs, founder).

The production was directed by Jade King Carroll. The dramaturg was Kristin Leahey. Scenic design was by Brittany Vasta. Lighting design was by Seth Reiser. Costume design was by Jen Caprio. Sound design was by Megumi Katayama and Fan Zheng, with original music by Fan Zheng. Projection design was by Kylee Loera. The assistant director was Britt Berke. The Italian pronunciation guide was by Alessandro Colla. The Latin pronunciation guide was by Professor Leah Whittington. The production stage manager was Alfredo Macias. The assistant stage manager was Abi Rowe.

The cast was as follows:

Judge / Priest	Carlo Albán
Artemisia Gentileschi	Kate Hamill
Orazio Gentileschi	Wynn Harmon
Agostino Tassi	Matthew Saldívar
Cosimo / Deputy	Jason O'Connell
Maria / Tuzia / Matteo	Joey Parsons

The Light and the Dark was additionally developed at the Eugene O'Neill Theater Center in Waterford, Connecticut.

THE LIGHT AND THE DARK

CHARACTERS

The play may be staged with two women and either three or four men. For five actors, the doubling should be as follows:

1. ARTEMISIA GENTILESCHI: Female-identifying. Deeply intelligent. Passionate. Determined. A fire within her. The same actor plays Artemisia at every age.
2. MARIA / TUZIA / MATTEO / MOTHER SUPERIOR: Female-identifying.
   MARIA, in her 20s–30s. A sex worker and art model. Deeply intelligent. Sees more than most.
   Doubles with TUZIA MEDAGLIA, in her 30s–40s. An impoverished widow seeking to come up in the world—resentful of the trials she's been through, and resentful of those who break the rules she's always had to follow.
   Doubles with MATTEO, a ten year-old boy. Serious. Wants to become a great artist. Not popular with his peers. Wants to do the right thing.
   Doubles with MOTHER SUPERIOR, a profoundly humorless woman of the cloth.
3. ORAZIO GENTILESCHI / DEPUTY: Male-identifying, 50+.
   ORAZIO: A painter from a long line of painters with talent. Wants to be one of the great masters. Very politick and cognizant of how he must not burn bridges in his small community of artists. Extremely fond of his daughter.
   DEPUTY: An officer of the court.
4. AGOSTINO TASSI: Male-identifying, 30s–40s. Charming and determined to succeed, with a storied past. Confident. Handsome. Truly believes he is the hero of the story. Truly believes he is the victim, when he is no longer the hero.
5. COSIMO / JUDGE / PRIEST: Male-identifying, 50+.
   COSIMO QUORLI: A short-tempered, opinionated, grandiloquent man, with great appetites. An expert appraiser of art. Bit of a pedant.

JUDGE: The richest person in the play—a nobleman, a man who truly believes he is fair and progressive, a modern man.
PRIEST: The voice of Church authority in the play. A holy man.

For six actors, the doubling should be as follows:

1. ARTEMISIA GENTILESCHI
2. MARIA / TUZIA / MATTEO
3. ORAZIO GENTILESCHI
4. AGOSTINO TASSI
5. COSIMO / DEPUTY
6. JUDGE / PRIEST

PLACE

Italy.

TIME

Early seventeenth century.

AUTHOR'S NOTES

This is not a play about a "rape victim." It is a play about a brilliant artist who happens to go through a series of brutal betrayals and uses her art, ultimately, to transcend her trauma. Please do not play the trauma at the beginning. Please do not telegraph the assault coming. Tonally, there is plenty of humor—do not lose the humor. She also need not be perfect, or gal-bossy; let her be quirky and imperfect and neurotic and ambitious and overconfident and driven and human. And please don't let her give up—she is a survivor.

As usual with my plays, I highly, HIGHLY, recommend incorporating modern elements along with the period—with music, with costumes, etc. Part of the point is that much of this story could—and still does—happen today.

The images of the paintings included here are not all the paintings that are mentioned, or which should be projected—just a smattering.

The translation of Tuzia's Italian on page 34 is as follows:
The nasty animal almost took off my fingers! Mother of God!

The translation of Agostino's tantrum on page 72 is as follows:
The little bitch! She's stolen the whole commission from me—they'll put up her panel instead of mine! What is this world coming to—that thieving shameless whore!

It is quite necessary that the actor playing Artemisia drives pace. Sorry about that, it is indeed exhausting! Rocket through at speed of thought in most places. It's how her brain works.

In the text of the play, a slash is used to indicate overlapping dialogue. Words in parentheses may or may not be spoken aloud.

"Papa" is pronounced "pa-PA."

ACT 1

1

[A large, blank wall serves as a projection screen. In front of it are the trappings of an art studio—drop cloths, stools, pots of pigment, brushes, rags. Fruit, flowers, a few jugs of water and wine; bread, olive oil. Many blank canvases.

It's all extremely simple. There's a stool, a couple of chairs. Something that might serve as a bed. Mirrors, positioned to catch the light.

ARTEMISIA, *any age, steps onstage; she is dressed simply, in a plain dress, wearing an apron stained with paint.*

She stops in front of a blank canvas on an easel—one that may, in fact, have no canvas in it at all. She has a stick of charcoal—ready to draft. She looks over her canvas, once twice—then, out at the audience—]

ARTEMISIA:
Composition, that's where you begin.
The story you want to tell.
It changes everything—your perspective—

And no one can dictate that to you.
No master can teach you how to start,
No matter what they may claim.
It can only come from your self.

So. Composition first—
The narrative focus, the angle of attack.
Once that has been worked out
With shadow and light—
and put in its different planes
All the rest is . . . [*she gets lost in it for a second*]!

. . . And the story I want to tell is . . .

Basta!
I must not get ahead of myself.
The story shall begin where I do—
I, I, I—
Born into this world Artemisia Gentileschi.
When I come squalling into the sweltering swamp air
Of Rome, 1593—
And survive long enough to have my name written in the baptismal books
I was named after Artemis—

[*Behind* ARTEMISIA *the painting* Diana, Huntress *by Bartolomeo Passerotti, 1551, appears.*]

Bartolomeo Passerotti, *Diana, Huntress,* 1550–1600. Oil on canvas.
Courtesy of Musée du Louvre, Paris.
https://collections.louvre.fr/en/ark:/53355/cl010059080.

ARTEMISIA:

The goddess of the hunt—the virgin—the butcher of men!
A scandalously pagan name, for a nice Catholic girl—
Don't you agree?

[*She indicates the painting behind her.*]

What, this? [*She "pfts" with horror*] This is not one of mine, yet—just wait.

My mother, Prudenzia, chose my name, Papa told me—
And he let her—since I was a girl and he was sure
That there would be sons after.
Poor, poor Papa.
And my poor mother, even more so.
She died in childbirth not a year after—
Trying to bring his boy into the world.

[*Behind* ARTEMISIA *appears on the wall a medieval icon of the Virgin Mary—*Madonna *by Lorenzo Monaco—as here:*]

Lorenzo Monaco, *Bust of Saint Mary (formerly entitled Madonna)*. Tempera on panel. Courtesy of Rijksmuseum, Amsterdam. https://id.rijksmuseum.nl/20025748.

ARTEMISIA:
The first image I remember as a child
Was the icon of the Virgin Mary on the wall—
Remote, benevolent, flat—
Staring mutely down upon our household.
And in my infant confusion
I thought that she was Prudenzia,
And I prayed to my sad-eyed, long-dead holy mother
Until she was forgotten entirely.
But who needs a mother
When your father is a God!
Artemis was born of Zeus
And my father was all divinity to me!
My father, Orazio Gentileschi!

2

[ORAZIO *steps upon the stage. About forty—ambitious, well-intentioned, fond of his daughter, beset by worries. He begins mixing a palette from pots of paint.*]

ARTEMISIA:
You see him, that handsome devil—?
I just thought he was—pure magic.
You see—my father was a painter
Making images of man—out of
horsehair and canvas and pigment!
I grew up crawling through his studio,
My clothes flecked with paint, stinking of liniment
The oils seeping into my pores!
[*gesturing to the studio around her*] I loved every inch of it—
The holy ground of his creation.
And not only was my father The Creator,
He was making art in a time when art was remaking the world

It was the Jubilee, the beginning of the seventeenth century, and my father's studio was in:

[*A view of Piazza di Spagna, 1600, flashes on the projection screen. City sounds fill the air—cursing in Italian, horses neighing, hooves on cobblestones.*]

ARTEMISIA:

ROME.

City built on ancient mores and rules, all broken a thousand times over—

Once the heart of the greatest empire in history,

And still the center of power and influence in all Europe!

A place where the greatest minds of the day meet and clash;

A place where the very image of humanity is being transformed!

Clement VIII is pope, now, and he knows the potential of imagery

To implant the messages of the church in hearts and in minds.

That, and the Protestants are getting a little bit too

Powerful speaking out against the dirty old systems.

He, and all the rest of the gentry of Europe—

Spend lavishly to awe and influence the masses.

Money, there's money flowing into the arts—

For once!

[*Image after image flashes on the projection screen—all the religious art of the exploding Italian Renaissance. Below the projection,* ORAZIO *begins to "paint" on a blank canvas, laying out lines carefully.*]

ARTEMISIA:

We are in a great rebirth!

Most of us peasants cannot read, or write, and will never travel far from where we are

Born— But—

Art teaches us who we are, who we might be!

Who is an angel, who is a devil—
Who is heroic, who is comic—
And, above it all, who holds the true power:
—our patrons, who buy themselves a slice of immortality.
Only Florence surpasses Rome in artistic reputation
—not that we would ever admit it to the Florentines.
It is a glorious time—as the world is being transformed—
—though it also is a dangerous time.
Heretics are burnt and citizens hanged for slight offenses—
and despite that, the streets are never safe—
Whenever morning hits the marble—
They find many bled to death in alleys, stabbed over vain nothings.

But I know nothing of that as a child!
I only know the safety of my father's studio
And inside—
Painters like him remake our sight!
You see—and let us use my Holy Mother to illustrate this point—

[ARTEMISIA *uses Monaco's painting* Madonna *to explain perspective.*]

For centuries images were mostly flat, like the Madonna here—
They were not supposed to represent the world around us, But rather something idealized.
You never believe this woman is standing before you, alive and breathing.
The painting does not pretend to be something more than a painting;
It lies lifeless upon the fresco.
Only to be worshipped, and never touched.

[*More images of the art of Michelangelo, Rafaello, Donatello, and Botticelli appear—particularly Raffaelo's* Madonna.]

Raphael (Raffaello Santi), *Madonna del Granduca,* ca. 1506–7.
Oil on panel. Palazzo Pitti, Galleria Palatina.
Photography: Gabinetto Fotografico delle Gallerie degli Uffizi.
https://www.uffizi.it/en/artworks/madonna-del-granduca.

ARTEMISIA:

Then, only recently—masters like Michelangelo, Rafaello, Botticelli came along
And taught us to view painting as an open window
Upon the world—to fix a vanishing point and compose
From there, so you paint as nature does
On a linear plane, adding depth and life.
It seems simple once explained—but that's what geniuses do
Break open our sight and make it look obvious.

And because it looks so obvious—
And because it's glamorous, and glorious.
The city is crawling with ambitious would-be artists
Looking to reshape the people's perspectives!
My father is one of the lucky ones, who makes a living doing it.
Orazio comes by it honestly—he's descended from a long line of painters
Was taught the trade carefully by
His father, and his father, and his father before him.
And, as the proud inheritor of that legacy—
My poor poor Papa—he is careful to play by all the rules.

[ORAZIO *turns around his blank canvas—and on the screen—we see Orazio's* The Lute Player *projected.*]

3

ORAZIO:

See, Misia, see—my newest!
The Lute Player!
Observe the proportions!

Orazio Gentileschi, *The Lute Player*, ca. 1612–20. Oil on canvas..
Courtesy of the National Gallery of Art, Washington, DC.

[*He points out on the painting:*]

The triangle is perfectly balanced here—
The top of the lute against the top of her head,
The curve of her elbow echoes the curve of the violin!

ARTEMISIA:

Orazio spends hours plotting out the math of every painting—the lines, the planes.

ORAZIO:

No sharp angles in her body—every brushstroke blended, so we know exactly what kind of music this lute will play, now don't we?
Soft. Subdued. Soothing.

ARTEMISIA:

He is nothing if not dedicated to the craft, and he wants

ORAZIO:

But I've taken a risk here—

ARTEMISIA:

Very badly to be great.

ORAZIO:

—did you catch it?!

ARTEMISIA:

A mannerist, they call him. A traditionalist, in his heart—

ORAZIO:

She's turned three-quarters away from the viewer! Unexpected, si?

ARTEMISIA:

—they do not always mean it kindly.

ORAZIO:

Well, Artemisia? You are seven now—old enough to judge for yourself. What do you think?

[ARTEMISIA, *looking at the audience, shifts into her younger self.*]

ARTEMISIA, AT 7:
Why isn't she reading the music, Papa?

ORAZIO:
What?

ARTEMISIA, AT 7:
The music is open, but she's not looking at it.

ORAZIO:
She is not meant to be a real musician, my Misia.

ARTEMISIA, AT 7:
No?

ORAZIO:
She is only a representation. The sheet music is merely a reference to a wider craft, like the other instruments— / and

ARTEMISIA, AT 7:
/ How does she play without looking?

ORAZIO:
I give her a downturned gaze, so we can see her modesty—we always demonstrate clarity of concept to patrons. A clue in every brushstroke, as to our intention.

ARTEMISIA, AT 7:
I still / don't—

ORAZIO:
/ [*riffing a bit*] She is not so much an ordinary woman as she is Harmonia—the muse of music. Or the Archetype of Melody, even, or—or—Grace.
—She may represent more than one ideal—as long as those ideals are elevated.

ARTEMISIA, AT 7:
Wut.

ORAZIO:
Perhaps you are too young to understand.

ARTEMISIA, AT 7:
Oh! Papa! The neck of the violin points at me—no matter where I stand!!!

ORAZIO:
Yes—yes!!!—it is all in the perspective!!!

[ARTEMISIA *hops around, trying perspectives, delighted.*]

ARTEMISIA, AT 7:
And here! And here! And here!

ORAZIO:
Well, Misia, what do you think? Is it a masterpiece?

ARTEMISIA, AT 7:
Bravo, Papa, bravo! You are a genius, bravo!

[ARTEMISIA *transforms back to her adult self as* ORAZIO *admires his painting.*]

ARTEMISIA:
Orazio makes a living.
But not a particularly comfortable one.
Probably even since the days of the cave-painters
There are always more hopeful artists
Then there are benefactors to commission.

ORAZIO:
You see the pile on the velvet, here, Misia—
And the sheen of her dress—that denotes silk.

ARTEMISIA:
It is a vicious ever-running war
To cultivate wealthy patrons.

ORAZIO:
Details, details, details—your choice in fabrics can lure in clients!

ARTEMISIA:
Even my father, gentle man, is not immune to the pressures of competition.

ORAZIO:
They will not have even a simulacrum of cheap linens in their palazzos!

ARTEMISIA:
Papa is a painter and makes his trade—

ORAZIO:
As my father always said, the vendor must know his market—
But—

ARTEMISIA:
But—

ORAZIO:
Still—our ideals—must overcome all other considerations.

ARTEMISIA:
When my father meets other artists in the street
—he must raise his hat first.

ORAZIO:
I really think—this may be my best work yet. Just wait until they see it!

ARTEMISIA, AT 7:
Who?

ORAZIO:

Them, Artemisia, the boys. The other members of the guild!
I can't wait to see their faces!

[*A church bell rings.*]

Come, child, come—we are going to be late!

4

ARTEMISIA:

Basta, yes, I am only a child.
What do I know?
I know that he takes
A blank canvas and creates life.
I worship him. And so I fashion myself in his image.
I am his second, his familiar, his sidekick.
And while I am young enough
Not to be thought of as a "woman"
I am allowed to tag along wherever he goes.
Hell, "woman"—what does that even mean?!
I never knew a lady except the widowed servingwoman Tuzia,
Who lives in the apartment upstairs and takes in our laundry and sometimes watches me
For a reduction in the rent.
I am something neither girl nor woman nor boy nor man,
I am only I, I, I, Artemisia.

And so this day, at seven years old, I, I, I am taken—
Across town with my father
Running flush with confidence in his latest creation—
To meet his colleague Cosimo Quorli,
And see a newly mounted altarpiece in the Contarelli Chapel,
-the source of much controversy.

[*Lights shift into Contarelli Chapel. Bells ring.* COSIMO*—a self-important man of huge appetites—waits. He is very irritated.* ORAZIO *hurries up, almost dragging* ARTEMISIA, AT 7. ORAZIO *is instinctively deferential to* COSIMO.]

ORAZIO:
Buongiorno, Cosimo!

COSIMO:
Buonasera, Orazio.

ORAZIO:
So, so, so sorry that we are late, my friend—but I was finishing my latest—you know how it is, when the Muse takes you, I really think that this work could be /

COSIMO:
—And you brought the girl, I see.

ORAZIO:
Oh. Yes. She has nowhere else to go. You're not too put out, are you?

COSIMO:
At you, Orazio—no. But at this world, wherein the wicked are rewarded more than the just?

ORAZIO:
What do you mean?

COSIMO:
Come see what that fucking lunatic has done now!

ARTEMISIA:
I am dragging my feet down the aisle of the new church.
Preparing to pour out a truly elaborate whine—
It is hot and dusty in here, and
Papa has dragged me all across town

Without even giving me my breakfast—
But just as I open my mouth to complain—
I look above the altar and I have no words—
For I see
My father is not the only God in this world.

[*An image of Caravaggio's* Judith Beheading Holofernes *appears behind them.*]

Caravaggio (Michelangelo Merisi), *Judith Beheading Holofernes*, ca. 1599–1600. Oil on canvas. Gallerie Nazionali di Arte Antica, Palazzo Barberini, Rome.

COSIMO [*spits*]:
Mother. Fucking. Caravaggio.

[ORAZIO, *wincing, tries to cover* ARTEMISIA*'s ears—but she steps forward, staring at the painting.*]

ARTEMISIA:
A century ago, there was Michelangelo, breaking the world open
By finding the angel in the marble.
And then all artists despaired after, for it seemed there was nothing new
Under the sun except found by his sight—and then a hundred years later
Caravaggio cracks their eyes open again!
And they all chase on behind!

COSIMO:
Paid twice what I was for the fresco. Bastardo.

ORAZIO:
—but this is—obscene. How can they display it at services?!!

ARTEMISIA:
Before Caravaggio painters
Started with the light.
Blank canvas, blank fresco,
And painted layers upon that blankness—
But Caravaggio starts in the darkness
And carves his way out from the shadows.

COSIMO:
They can't.

ARTEMISIA:
The dark defines the light; the light defines the dark!
Look at his colors, at his depth

Look how he embraces the violence
And rejects the sanitized ideal.

COSIMO:
Certainly nothing fucking subtle about it, is there? Fucking show-off!

ARTEMISIA:
When Caravaggio shows murder, he includes the blood.
When Caravaggio paints fruit, he depicts the rot.

ORAZIO:
Will he have to return the commission?

COSIMO:
Oh, no, no! The patron is going to add it to his private collection!
And commissioned three more!

ORAZIO:
But it's—not at all what clients request.

COSIMO:
He teaches the money set what they want! The rules never apply to fucking Michele, now do they?!!

ORAZIO:
—we ought to talk to the guild.

COSIMO:
Why? What does he care, if we throw him out? The son of a bitch is getting rich.

ARTEMISIA, AT 7 [*re: the painting*]:
Who is this lady, Papa?

ORAZIO:
This is—Judith and Holofernes, child—

[ARTEMISIA *looks at him blankly.*]

A Bible story. The details don't matter.

COSIMO:
You neglect her education, Orazio.
Come here, girl.

[*He maneuvers* ARTEMISIA *very close to him; it's uncomfortable.*]

Judith was a Hebrew widow, you see—from Bethulia, do you know where that is?

ARTEMISIA, AT 7:
No.

COSIMO:
Mm. And Holofernes here—was a general from Assyria, do you know about that?

ARTEMISIA, AT 7:
No.

COSIMO:
Then you don't know much, do you?

ARTEMISIA, AT 7:
No. So why is she stabbing him?

COSIMO:
Because this Holofernes wants to invade her city, and murder all her friends and family, and ravage all their wives and daughters—

ORAZIO:
Cosimo—

COSIMO:
But this Judith is a very pretty little thing, you see? So she talks her way into Holofernes's tent by implying she'll do all sorts of pretty little things for him, and she fills up his cup with wine and gives him many kisses and caresses and probably a taste of her pretty little—

ORAZIO
Cosimo, *please*—

COSIMO:
And just when he's very relaxed and drunk and sleepy, as all men become after such delights, she calls in her old hag of a maidservant here—and takes up his nasty sharp sword and saws off his big ugly head [*demonstratively*] GLAHHHHH.

ORAZIO [*trying to save it*]:
And the point is—she saved her city, Misia. And everyone inside it.

ARTEMISIA:
Her face, Papa—she doesn't want to do it.

ORAZIO:
No. See how daintily she holds the knife?
She looks like a real lady.

COSIMO:
Heard the model was some whore from the taverna. [*He spits*]
He just didn't paint the rash!

ORAZIO:
Shh. Cosimo. [*Gesturing to* ARTEMISIA] She is too young for such things!

COSIMO:
Then why the fuck is she out with you?!!

ORAZIO:
If you could please just—watch your language—

COSIMO:
Fuck that fuck that fuck that!

ORAZIO:
We are in a church!

COSIMO:
For fuck's sake, Orazio, this is a real fucking crisis!
This vulgar little turd is going to take all of our commissions and suck all of the fucking air out of fucking Rome, and you want me to watch my fucking mouth because of your brat?!
Get! yourself! a fucking! nanny!!!!

[*He slams out—pausing only to cross himself at the altar.*]

ARTEMISIA, AT 7 [*experimentally*]:
"Fuck."

ORAZIO:
Shh. Misia. Do not say that word.

ARTEMISIA, AT 7:
You let your friend say it!

ORAZIO [*sighing*]:
—He—is well placed with every patron in the city.

ARTEMISIA, AT 7:
What does that mean?

ORAZIO:
Artists—real artists—are a small tribe. We must get along, to get ahead.

ARTEMISIA, AT 7:
Can I meet the artist that painted this, Papa?

ORAZIO:
NO! Michele Caravaggio—a bad man, Misia. Runs in the wrong crowd, violent and dissolute and, well, you can see from—his work. [*Gesturing to the painting distastefully*]
[*Sighing heavily*] But, scandal—is—sometimes profitable.

ARTEMISIA, AT 7:
—I thought anybody who could make this must be—wonderful.

ORAZIO:
This? . . . This will be forgotten, as all cheap infamies are. Besides—I have painted much the same subject.
I wonder when Cosimo will come and see my *Lute Player*?

[ARTEMISIA *turns back into her adult self.*]

ARTEMISIA:
After the disappointment is managed—the *Lute Player* will set no records for price, will cause no profitable scandals—
Papa drags out of storage just to show me—his *Judith and Holofernes.*

[*Orazio's* Judith and Her Maidservant with the Head of Holofernes *is projected next to Caravaggio's.*]

Caravaggio (Michelangelo Merisi), *Judith Beheading Holofernes,* ca. 1599–1600. Oil on canvas. Gallerie Nazionali di Arte Antica, Palazzo Barberini, Rome.

Orazio Gentileschi, *Judith and Her Maidservant with the Head of Holofernes*, 1621–24. Oil on canvas. Wadsworth Atheneum Museum of Art, Hartford, CT, 1949.52. Photography: Allen Phillips / Wadsworth Atheneum.

ARTEMISIA:

Look at my poor Papa's work, next to the master's. Careful, inoffensive—and flat.

ORAZIO:

Well, Artemisia? What d'you think—am I not the equal of a Caravaggio?
. . . Misia?

ARTEMISIA, AT 7:

Papa . . . .

I really miss the stabbing.

ARTEMISIA:

Orazio is right, I am getting old enough for opinions.
And with this first, minor betrayal—
This first separation from my Holy Father—
He begins to see me as not quite his familiar, anymore.

ORAZIO:

Artemisia—I have been thinking—it is time for you to get an education.

5

[*Back at the Gentileschis' studio—1601.* ARTEMISIA *is in full tantrum.*]

ARTEMISIA, AT 8:

NOoooOOOOO! NO PAPA NO PAPA NO!

ORAZIO:

There's no use crying, Artemisia. Tuzia has already packed you a bag.

[TUZIA, *the servingwoman, desperate and not self-reflective, puts a few last little items into a canvas bag, as:*]

ARTEMISIA, AT 8:
WHY must you send me to live in the church!

ORAZIO:
Not in the church, dear heart, in the nunnery.

ARTEMISIA, AT 8:
NOOOOOOOOOO!

TUZIA:
Jesu, those lungs. Sure you don't want to send her to the opera?

[ARTEMISIA *wails, loudly.*]

ORAZIO:
Thank you, Tuzia—she will be fine—

TUZIA [*as* ARTEMISIA *wails, loudly.*]:
Young ladies are often sent away, my Signorina—

[ARTEMISIA *wails, loudly.*]

—without having such carryings-on—

[ARTEMISIA *wails, loudly.*]

ORAZIO:
Thank you, Tuzia—if we could just have a moment—

[ARTEMISIA *wails, loudly.*]

TUZIA [*brushing past* ORAZIO]:
Let me, Signore Gentileschi.
Quiet, child, quiet! You hear me? HUSH!

[*She gives* ARTEMISIA*'s face a little firm shake; the crying pauses for a moment. Then, triumphantly to* ORAZIO:]

There. Now was that so very . . . [ARTEMISIA *bites her*] OW!

ORAZIO:
THANK you, Tuzia! That will be all!

TUZIA [*clutching her bitten hand*]:
Just wait till the nuns get their hands on you!

[ARTEMISIA *wraps herself around her father's leg, crying, as* TUZIA *exits with the bag; cursing to herself, angrily:*]

Il brutto animaletto mi ha quasi tolto le dita! Madre di Dio!

[ORAZIO, *ineffectively, tries to pry* ARTEMISIA *from his leg, as:*]

ORAZIO
Misia—Artemisia. Please. I don't know how to raise a girl properly. If you were a boy—

ARTEMISIA, AT 8:
Let me be a boy, then! I can be a boy! A better boy than any of the 'prentices, I'm smarter, and I'm stronger—I thumped Giancarlo just the other day!

ORAZIO:
—you need a real education. Don't you want to learn to sew—[*she sobs*] or to make pretty music [*she sobs harder*]—or at least to read and to write?

ARTEMISIA, AT 8:
Why should I ever toreadandtowrite!

ORAZIO:
Oh / Misia.

ARTEMISIA, AT 8:
/ Papa—I only want to be like you!

ORAZIO:
You can be much greater than me, sweetheart. Think, if I build a big enough fortune and you mark the sisters well enough—you

may be a fine lady—the wife or the mother of the great artist of tomorrow!

ARTEMISIA, AT 8:
I don't want to be a lady! I am I, your Artemisia. And I want to be a painter!

[TUZIA *appears again; she looks at him, meaningfully.*]

ORAZIO:
I've been selfish—keeping you with me for so long. But you must accept the compromises of this world. We both must.

TUZIA:
Come, you little hellion—the mother superior is at the gate.

[TUZIA *takes her arm and begins to drag her away*—ARTEMISIA *cries.*]

ARTEMISIA, AT 8:
Papa, PAPA! PLEASE! Please don't send me away.

ORAZIO:
Misia—do stop crying.
You know how much it pains me.

[ORAZIO *turns back to his painting, as* ARTEMISIA *transitions back into her adult self.*]

6

[*Church bells ring in the distance as we slowly transition to the cold stone of the nunnery.*]

ARTEMISIA:
Poor poor Papa vastly overcredits
The education offered at the nunnery.

They don't teach much in the way of reading, or writing
To any of the little girls, scrubbed and stuffed into novice's linens.
Fear, fear, fear—
Is the first and last lesson—
From the grim-faced nuns, with their interminable droning Latin!

[A PRIEST *stands up upon a dias; he is lit like a saint.*]

[*The* MOTHER SUPERIOR, *50s, fully outfitted in habit, merciless—enters—and forces* ARTEMISIA *to kneel as they pray:*]

PRIEST:

Miserere mei, Deus: secundum
magnam misericordiam
tuam. / Et secundum multi-
tudinem miserationum tua-
rum, dele iniquitatem meam.
Quoniam iniquitatem meam ego
cognosco: et peccatum meum
contra me est semper.

ARTEMISIA:

/ Have mercy upon me, O God:
after Thy great goodness.
Wash me thoroughly from my
wickedness: and cleanse me
from my iniquity.
For I acknowledge my faults: and
my sin
is ever before me!

ARTEMISIA:

Ooo I hate it. I hate it so motherfucking much.
Thrust from a world of only men into one of only women
I belong to neither.
And I'm, uhm, unpopular, with the other girls at the nunnery—
The future wives and mothers of the creators of tomorrow—
They stare and whisper behind my back.
I do not eat right, or sit right—I certainly do not speak right.
Not as my long-forgotten mother would have.
—I am always getting into trouble.
I am lectured and prayed over.
I am strapped and switched.
And I waste a year, wearing my knees raw with kneeling, on that fucking cold stone church floor

Staring at the nunnery's ugly, amateurish altarpiece painting of priggish Saint Paul,
Who preached that women should be subordinate to their husbands—
Reciting my miseries over and over again!

PRIEST:
Cor mundum crea in me, Deus: et spiritum rectum innova in visceribus meis. Ne proiicias me a facie tua: et spiritum sanctum tuum ne auferas a me.

ARTEMISIA:
Make me a clean heart, O God: Cast me not away from Thy presence!
For a broken and contrite heart, O God, shalt Thou not despise!
[*ironically*] Miserere mei, Deus!

ARTEMISIA:

[*As she speaks, she begins smearing her hands with something black and sticky.*]

But I've come to it too late.
I learned too much, trailing in my father's wake.
I saw that to flout the foolish rules of this world—You sometimes, must simply—go bigger!

7

MOTHER SUPERIOR [*screaming at the top of her lungs*]:
TARRRRRRRRRR!

[*And BAM—we slam back into the studio as* MOTHER SUPERIOR *bodily throws* ARTEMISIA, *aged 9, in front of her father.*]

THE TAR, SIGNORE! TAR EVERYWHERE! WE NEVER SHALL BE RID OF IT!

ORAZIO:
Signora, / what is

MOTHER SUPERIOR:
/ TAKE HER BACK THIS INSTANT! AND LOCK HER AWAY AT ONCE! AND SUFFER NONE TO EVER AGAIN HEAR HER SPEAK!

ORAZIO:
If you will only explain—

MOTHER SUPERIOR:
We have known wicked children before, Signore. We have seen young sinners of every kind, and never failed in putting them on the path to salvation! But I swear to you now, that if this creature crosses our threshold again, we shall go directly to the highest authorities, and you will see her prosecuted as a heretic!

ORAZIO:
Signora, signora—please! She is just a little girl—

[*The* MOTHER SUPERIOR *whirls out—but just as she does:*]

MOTHER SUPERIOR:
A girl. A GIRL?! No, I tell you now that she is a SUCCUBUS—A LILITH—A SLATTERNLY LITTLE HELLSMOUTH DAUGHTER OF A WITCH—

ORAZIO:
/ Really—

MOTHER SUPERIOR:
/ FOR WHAT SORT OF A FREAKISH DEVIL, SIR—WOULD PAINT AN ALTAR BLACK?!

[*She slams out, crossing herself frantically—or perhaps making the sign of the evil eye against Misia. Beat.*]

ARTEMISIA, AT 9:
I didn't want to use tar, Papa. But I had no soot, for pigment.
And I didn't like their altar painting. And I could do much better.
And I thought—
That I should carve it out of the dark.

ORAZIO:
Misia—

ARTEMISIA, AT 9:
I would have done it, too, if they hadn't interrupted me
With all of their stupid screaming!

ORAZIO:
Misia.

ARTEMISIA:
I don't like Saint Paul. [*Very fast*] I was going to paint Saint Margaret instead— because she fought a dragon, and told that girl Joan
To free all of France, a hundred years ago. Isn't that right?

ORAZIO:
Misia—you cannot grow up in—in my studio, with the men. It is not appropriate, and—
You cannot learn a lady's trade from me.

ARTEMISIA AT 9:
This is my trade!!
Teach me how to do what you do!!!
Papa—make me an apprentice!!!!

ORAZIO [*trying to be resolute*]:
If the world was different—

ARTEMISIA AT 9:
You can make it different!
You can!
Isn't that what the masters do?

ORAZIO:
It would be a scandal!

ARTEMISIA AT 9:
You said that scandal is profitable!

ORAZIO:
For Caravaggio!

ARTEMISIA AT 9:
And aren't you as great as the great Caravaggio?
Papa—do not send me away.
[*This is a threat*] Or I shall have to dare bigger.

[*Beat.*]

ORAZIO:
Child, you do not need an education. You need an exorcism.

[ARTEMISIA *chuckles.*]

Oh, my Artemisia—
You know how it pains me to deny you.

[*She jumps up and hugs him.*]

8

ARTEMISIA:
Is there any time happier than this?!!!
The time when I begin to learn the trade
That was my father's, and my father's before him,
And perhaps I really was made in man's own image
Because for the first time in my life—
I fall desperately in love—
—*with my craft!*

Please, the boys of the studio
Are nothing to me, compared to the sheer pleasure
Of the *work*.
Even though it is hard, that work!
They start you from the bottom
No matter who your father is. [*Very fast:*]
First, they have you cleaning the studio, sweeping and dusting
Washing the rags, and wiping the brushes, till
You're deemed not quite too stupid to learn to build the frames
Upon which you'll learn to stretch the canvas, and once you've
    learned that
They'll put you to whittling charcoal, and pasting in horsehairs
Till your vision goes all swimming—and then you must learn—
To pound the pigments, first the cheaper ones—
The blacks, the reds, and finally
Graduating to the ultramarine blues and golds so precious that if
You spill a drop, you'll get a beating—
The blue's worth more than your blood!

And when, after the years, your hands go raw and then get coarse,
And when your muscles ache and then get strong
And when you know every step of the process from beginning
Till you could do it in your sleep, till you could teach
Even the dullest 'prentice boy how to do every step
So nothing of our craft may be lost over the years—
Then! Only then!
You may pick up the brush!

[ORAZIO *hands her a brush.*]

Fifteen years old, and finally—finally.
I may begin to paint!
I want to attack the huge canvases immediately,
The frescoes, the murals—the biggest stories,
I, I, I — !!!!

ORAZIO:
Slow, slow, Misia! You are not ready—

ARTEMISIA:
I am, though, Papa, I will take on anything,

ORAZIO:
Not until your maestro says you can.
Compromise, my girl—you must accept the compromises of this world.

ARTEMISIA:
My father is the master and I the apprentice.
So.
I start as he tells me to.
First you paint
Just
Shapes.
Still lifes.
Landscapes.
Flowers. Shells. Fruits. Flowers. Shells. Fruits. Flowers. Shells,
Fruits—
I think if I see another apple I will puke—
For a full year I do this,
Until my father judges my work sufficient, and says that I may graduate—
From flowers to fruits to *flesh!*

[ORAZIO *takes a look and nods approvingly*—ARTEMISIA *celebrates as the lights change.*]

Yes! You'll see.
I AM SO EXCITED.
So eager to start that my hands shake!!!
Today is my first real class!
Today is the day I begin to become a *maestro*—
And I am not alone!

I am joined by other apprentices
Who made their way from canvas to frame to brush to here!
All men, of course, although "men" is a broad term—
"Boys" is better.
Only one we may say is a "man."
He's grown, almost a compatriot of my father's—
Here only to do the finishing touches on his education.
I am sixteen years old. Today is the glorious day I have been working towards—
For years and years—
And today is when I meet—
Agostino Tassi.

9

[*Back in the studio—a master class is about to be taught. We hear the sound of boys setting up their easels, low murmurs.*]

[ORAZIO *has just clapped the back of* AGOSTINO TASSI. AGOSTINO *is handsome; charming, when he wants to be. He has a long and storied past. He truly thinks of himself as the hero of any story.*]

ORAZIO:
Agostino—this is my daughter, Artemisia Gentileschi.

AGOSTINO:
Ah! Buongiorno, bella Signora.

[*He bows to* ARTEMISIA*—takes her hand to kiss, politely.*]

I see the resemblance, of course.

ORAZIO:
She'll be joining us in studio today.

AGOSTINO:
Oh. Will she now. Will she indeed.

ARTEMISIA [*to the audience*]:
Flowers to fruits—to flesh!

[MARIA, *a figure model, quite beautiful, walks through the class; she is wearing only a robe. A chorus of whistles accompanies her—low male murmurs and chuckles.*]

ORAZIO:
Boys! Boys. [*Remembering himself*] And—Misia. None of that, in here.

AGOSTINO:
Can you blame them, Orazio?

ARTEMISIA:
"Orazio," he says.

AGOSTINO:
Cooped up with canvases all day long—and you remember being that young—the blood never reaches your brain.

ORAZIO:
Still—gentlemen. This is a classroom, not a brothel.

AGOSTINO:
Of course. [*He winks.*]

ARTEMISIA:
The boys all love him.
I wish I could say I was more perceptive.
I wish I could say I hate Agostino, right off. But the truth is—

AGOSTINO [*to* MARIA]:
Ciao, Principessa.

ARTEMISIA:
He's got a certain appeal.

[AGOSTINO *positions* MARIA*'s stool, dusts it off—bows to her.*]

AGOSTINO:
Your humble throne awaits.

[MARIA, *pointedly, repositions the stool.*]

ARTEMISIA:
He's new to my father's studio—

AGOSTINO:
My heavens, if I were a younger man.

ARTEMISIA:
He speaks of a colorful past.

AGOSTINO [*re* MARIA]:
When I was so young—I "befriended" a girl like that once, Orazio—

ARTEMISIA:
Get him in his cups, and the boys say he'll talk of time spent as a prisoner on the galleys—punishment over some unnamed offense—but somehow secured himself a pardon.

AGOSTINO:
And she had such a mouth on her! Such a mouth—*ohhh* [*he laughs*]

ARTEMISIA:
And it's not so hard to believe.

AGOSTINO [*clapping* ORAZIO *on the back*]:
I'll tell you all about it another time.

ARTEMISIA:
He's good at ingratiating himself with both low and high. Moves in monied circles. Says he knows the Medicis, hints he may even be the bastard of a noble himself. And because he's got those connections, and opportunities are precious, my father—

ORAZIO:
Agostino, if you will—

ARTEMISIA:
Always playing the game—

AGOSTINO:
Of course. Your floor, maestro!

ARTEMISIA:
Appears to find him absolutely—

AGOSTINO:
Boys. Listen up!
One of the greats is speaking!

ARTEMISIA:
—charming.

ORAZIO [*smiling*]:
Ah, well. Thank you, thank you, my friend. Our subject today for composition, gentlemen—and Misia—shall be Susanna and the Elders.

[ARTEMISIA *snaps into the scene.*]

ARTEMISIA:
Really? That's where we're beginning?

ORAZIO:
It is by retracing the classics that we discover mastery. Like Christ and the father, imitation is the source of innovat / (ion)

ARTEMISIA:
/ But that old chestnut?

ORAZIO:
Artemisia! [*A pause, then—*] Meditate, boys, on the lady in her garden, shielded from prying eyes—high walls around her, kept innocent and safe—

[MARIA *sits on the stool. She carefully arranges her area.*]

ARTEMISIA:
Another Bible story.
This time, I am a little less ignorant.

ORAZIO:
None but her husband has ever seen her charms, but as two men peer over the walls—

ARTEMISIA:
It has been done and redone, done and redone.

ORAZIO:
They find temptation therein!

ARTEMISIA:
What new thing could ever be found in this:

ORAZIO:
Susanna and the Elders—go.

[MARIA *drops her robe.*]

ARTEMISIA:
Whoa.

AGOSTINO:
I am surprised, Orazio—to see this kind of study here.

ARTEMISIA:
I've never seen another girl naked before!

ORAZIO:
Caravaggio uses live models.

ARTEMISIA:
And as I try mightily to seem impassive—not to stare too hard, I feel

AGOSTINO:
Carvaggio is an infamy. And currently, I believe, on the lam.

ARTEMISIA:
The eyes of the class upon *me*—

ORAZIO:
Even if he is a scandal—there are still things we can learn.

ARTEMISIA:
One set of eyes, in particular.

AGOSTINO:
—Orazio. I ask as a friend. Is it really right—that your daughter should be here?

ARTEMISIA:
Why—why should't I be? /

AGOSTINO:
/ Is it really appropriate?

ARTEMISIA:
It's much less of a mystery
To me than to any of you!

ORAZIO:
It is part of her training, Agostino.

AGOSTINO:
—It's just—the boys, eh? They may get some ideas—

ARTEMISIA:
Women have painted nudes before—
Diana Scultori! Fede Galizia! Lavinia Fontana—

AGOSTINO:
—and I believe those were all women married, widows and wives, not maids of what, sixteen—?

ARTEMISIA:
I deserve to be here just as much as any other <u>fucking apprentice</u>!

ORAZIO:
Artemisia! *Language!*
Agostino, thank you for your concern—
But she has been promised a chance.

AGOSTINO:
Of course, Maestro. Fathers and their little girls—the bond is very strong.

ORAZIO:
Students, begin.
[*Privately to* ARTEMISIA:] Misia. No more outbursts, you hear me?
[*To the room in general:*] Start.

ARTEMISIA:
It's now, now, now, or never.
After I've offered battle like Saint Margaret,
I must defeat the dragon.
I look at my stretched canvas—
At my pigments, slowly drying.
At the girl—seemingly trying not to breathe.
Everyone else's charcoal is already scratching—
And I wonder if every boy in here—
Thinks that blankness will defeat me!
—And I just, I just feel . . .

ORAZIO [*to the room*]:
Squint first, to see the big shapes, eh? Broad ideas—lights and darks—and then details.

ARTEMISIA:
Fear, fear, fear—
That's the lesson they want to teach me!
And I—I—I—

[*She takes a deep breath.*]

Basta.
Composition!

[ORAZIO *lightly, nonsexually touches* MARIA *as he speaks, demonstrating.*]

ORAZIO:
Note how the light bounces from the color of cloth behind her, which reflects onto her skin—and her shadow contains a hint of her skin's tones, echoed back—how they are all interconnected!

ARTEMISIA:
Composition, that's where you begin.
The lines, the planes, the perspective—
And my perspective is . . . ???

ORAZIO:
The focus of the gaze defines form, my boys—defines everything.

ARTEMISIA [*urgently trying to find her way into the story. All of this is VERY fast:*]
. . . In the Bible, the Book of Daniel, Susanna
Is a beautiful young woman bathing in her garden
And two men spy upon her.
And when she turns and sees the perverts
They try to bribe her into
Having relations with them—
And when she refuses, they
Say they'll accuse her of adultery—
Say that they saw her lying down
With some random man—
Which means that she'll go with any man, that she's loose
Which means she'll be stoned to death—

With full approval of the law, and in the public square.
Eventually, Daniel swoops in and testifies to her character—
Which means she is saved, during her trial—
But we are not painting the trial, we are painting
The moment that Susannah is surprised by the elders—!

ORAZIO:
Switch positions.

[MARIA *shifts, as:*]

ARTEMISIA:
And
The story I want to tell—is—
What I want to—tell . . . is—???
I. I. I!

I pick up my charcoal.
I begin to sketch.
And.

Something *happens.*
She is she—but she is also—
More than she.
Flowers, shells, fruits
Flowers, shells, fruits
Flowers, shells—
In the downy curve of her cheek—the peach!
In the slight rise of her veins—the stem of the flower—
In the soft curl of her fingers—the shell.
I have never seen a human body like this before
As a compendium of nature's wonders
I see my father's wisdom in forcing me to paint endless chaste still lifes
There is a sacred symmetry here!

I sketch this young woman I see before me—
E bravo—brava—I create life!

ORAZIO:
Switch positions.

[MARIA *shifts, as:*]

ARTEMISIA:
Well.
Kind of.
I'm not a master yet.
I make mistakes.
I smudge and erase with gum and start over.
But still—there is a line, a gesture—
And as I sketch, I feel
Not as if I am narrating the story, but
That I am . . . listening.
To not only her body—but
My body, God's creation!
My body knows what to do!
I feel as if sunlight is just flowing
From above and I know
The divine speaks through my hands
More than through any priest's droning Latin!
I only need get out of its way!
And when I can simply let it take over-
I go into a sort of—
It is—silent, in my head.
My racing thoughts stop—
I slip into a stream and am washed away.
I look up and hours have gone by.
I have mixed pigments and started painting, all in
A trance, such as saints have

Or a fit of madness
But look what I—
I can make! I! I! I!

ORAZIO:
Switch positions.

[MARIA *shifts, as:*]

[*A projection of Artemisia's* Susanna and the Elders *appears on screen behind her, as she furiously paints.*]

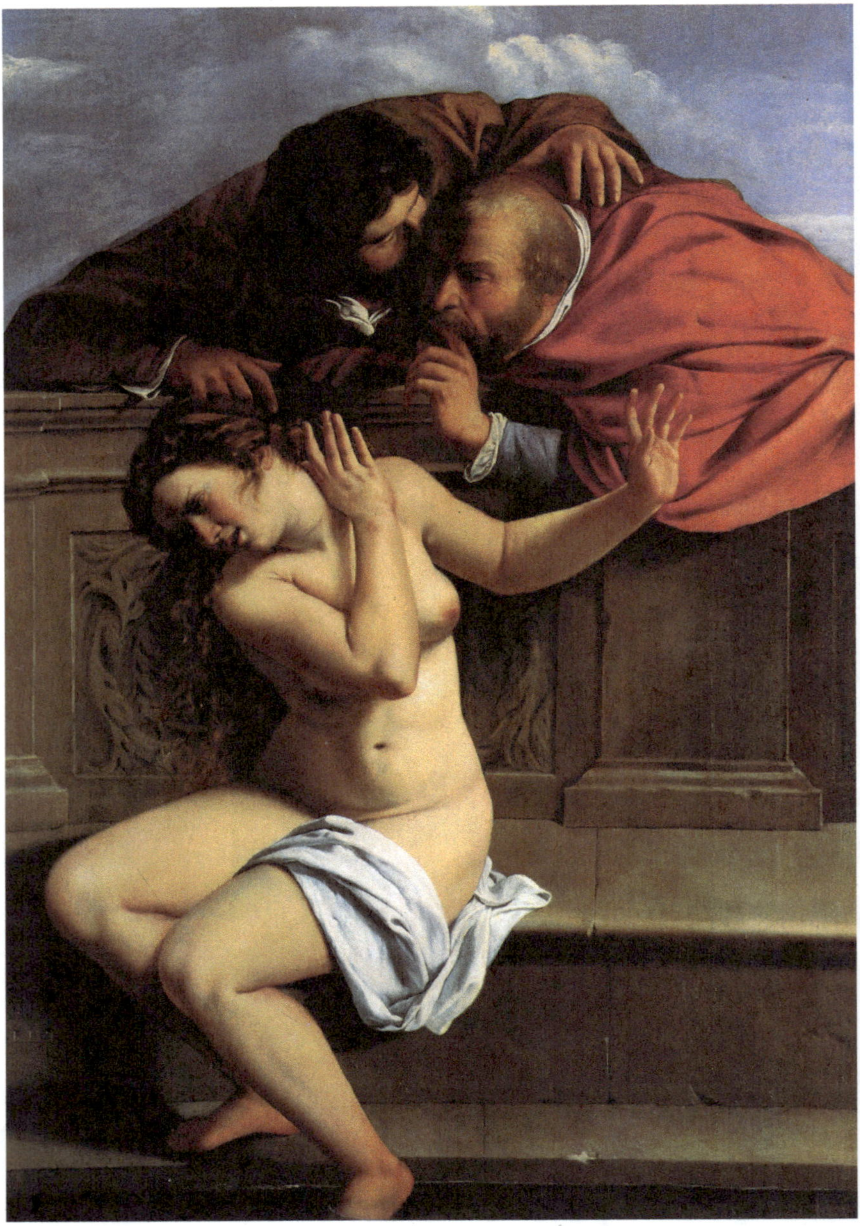

Artemisia Gentileschi, *Susanna and the Elders,* 1610. Oil on canvas.
Courtesy of the Schönborn Collection, Pommersfelden.

ARTEMISIA:

To paint the subject, you must become the subject
To depict Susanna, you must feel as she does
Feel her own terror in your muscles
Her own breath in your chest
Myself and the brush, the pigment, the canvas
It all is swept together
Toward this transfiguration
And the only thing that can break this flawless revery is—!

AGOSTINO:

Pst. *Pst.* Can I help you?

ARTEMISIA:

—Excuse me?

AGOSTINO:

Come. Let me help you.

ARTEMISIA:

What?

AGOSTINO:

Let me give you a few pointers.

ARTEMISIA:

Shouldn't we all be working?

AGOSTINO:

I am practiced enough, Principessa. I don't need studio time. Hm. You have some talent, you know.

ARTEMISIA:

Thank you—!

AGOSTINO:

But your perspective is off.

ARTEMISIA:
Excuse me?

AGOSTINO:
You need to reexamine your proportions.

ARTEMISIA:
My proportions are—perfect.

AGOSTINO:
Are they, now. [*He laughs*] You'll see.
Orazio—we should take a break, don't you think?

ORAZIO:
Oh—yes—yes, that's—boys, go stretch, have some water. [*To* MARIA] And you, too—

MARIA:
Maria.

ORAZIO:
Maria. Feel free to move about. You may wish to, ah—cover up.

MARIA:
Can *I* have some water?

ORAZIO:
Oh—of course. But do be back soon.

[MARIA *gets off of the stool—but does not go far. She overhears most of this:*]

AGOSTINO:
Orazio. Maestro di tutto! Won't you come and see—your precocious child's work?

ORAZIO:
Ah, Misia. Yes—let us—let us. [*He inspects* ARTEMISIA*'s painting.*] Oh. Mm.

ARTEMISIA [*confidently*]:
And so, Papa? Have I not done you proud?

ORAZIO:
It is—Interesting, my dear. But—we must consider the framing carefully.

ARTEMISIA:
I *did.* I *have*. You see—as with your lute player, there is a triangle here—her ear, and her hand, and his mouth—

ORAZIO:
Ah—but your triangle is not balanced.

AGOSTINO:
It is all Susanna—and no elders.

ARTEMISIA:
She's the center of the story!

AGOSTINO:
And what a center you've made her.

ARTEMISIA:
What does that mean?

AGOSTINO:
All these stray hairs. The dimples in her thighs. Stretch marks.

ARTEMISIA:
God gave her stretch marks. I am painting what I see.

ORAZIO:
The best art is more about ideal proportions.

[ARTEMISIA *looks at him blankly.*]

We need to create that which surpasses reality.

ARTEMISIA:
More than God's reality?

ORAZIO:

—It's not just that. It's the—the tone, my love. There's no coyness, no delicacy in this lady. No—no sensuality. She looks—

ARTEMISIA:

Horrified?!!! Yes. These men are threatening to ravish her! Why wouldn't she be—

AGOSTINO [*to* ORAZIO, *over her head*]:

Orazio. She does not understand the context.

ORAZIO:

Our clients want works to enlighten: entertain, not disturb.

ARTEMISIA:

Caravaggio painted his fruit rotting.

ORAZIO:

There is a long tradition—of this particular subject as a kind of—of—celebration of the female body.

ARTEMISIA:

. . . So then our patrons are the elders?

ORAZIO:

No, no—you are so young still, child, perhaps you do not understand.

AGOSTINO:

Perhaps if you were shown an example.

[AGOSTINO *indicates his canvas—and Tintoretto's* Susanna and the Elders*—the one currently displayed in the Louvre—flashes on the screen.*]

Tintoretto (Jacopo Robusti), *Susanna at Her Bath*, ca. 1550–75.
Oil on canvas. Courtesy of Musée du Louvre, Paris. Copyright © 2025
GrandPalaisRmn (musée du Louvre) / Mathieu Rabeau.
https://collections.louvre.fr/en/ark:/53355/cl010062254.

ORAZIO:

Ah, this is very nice, Agostino, very nice indeed.

AGOSTINO:

À la Tintoretto.

ORAZIO:

Of course, yes, I saw that at once.

AGOSTINO:

See, Signora Gentileschi—her coy positioning! The tempting smile, the knowing way she looks at the viewer, almost gloating in her power, revelling in being watched!

She's inviting—irresistible—the quintessential portrait of forbidden lust.

ARTEMISIA:

She just looks uncomfortable to me.

ORAZIO:

Misia—

ARTEMISIA:

Who would sit like that? Why is she twisted around in this completely awkward, half teeter-totter position? What woman has ever sat stark naked, splay-legged, thrusting her sweaty pelvis into the faces of her fully clothed servants, and smirked the whole time like a self-satisfied village idiot? WHO. THE FUCK. IS SHE LOOKING AT?!!!

ORAZIO:

Artemisia! You are becoming—much too emotional!!!!!!

Apologize at once.

AGOSTINO:

No need.

Do not take me amiss, Signora Gentileschi. I only wanted to help.

ORAZIO:
You are kind to say so, Agostino. But if my daughter cannot learn respect—she will not be allowed to learn with the others.

[*Beat.*]

ARTEMISIA:
Mi dispiace, Signore Tassi. It shall not happen again.

[MARIA *clears her throat.*]

ORAZIO:
Ah, back, are you—

MARIA:
Maria.

ORAZIO:
Maria, of course! Let me call in the boys.

[ORAZIO *leaves.* ARTEMISIA, *angrily, turns back to her canvas.*]

AGOSTINO:
You know, Signora Gentileschi, whatever you may believe—I am a great supporter of women. And if you ever did want my guidance . . .

ARTEMISIA:
. . . what could *I* ever learn from *you?*

AGOSTINO:
—you may be surprised.

ARTEMISIA:
I don't think so, Signore. You got her spine [*she counts quickly 1-2-3-4*] four vertebrae too long.

[AGOSTINO *balks, then smiles, angrily—sweeps a bow and goes back to his canvas. As he does,* MARIA *sidles up behind* ARTEMISIA*—looks at her canvas, over her shoulder.*]

MARIA:
You know—you might have asked me.

[ARTEMISIA, *in shock, looks around—she's not talking to anybody else.*]

ARTEMISIA:
. . . Um. What?

MARIA:
What I thought. About what Susanna feels. I'm her, after all. Aren't I?

ARTEMISIA:
Oh.

MARIA:
—So?

ARTEMISIA:
So. Um. What do you think—that—Susanna feels?

MARIA [*still looking pointedly only at the painting*]:
That men are dangerous; that their desires are dangerous. And thwarted men—men of pride—are most dangerous of all.
I like the stretch marks, for the record. I did earn them.

[ARTEMISIA *stares at her, blankly.*]

You should have asked.

[ORAZIO *bustles back in.* MARIA *sails away from* ARTEMISIA.]

ORAZIO:
All right, boys, get settled.
Now, young lady—

MARIA [*very annoyed*]:
Maria.

ORAZIO:
Mm—of course—[*guiding* MARIA *to her chair*] If you will sit, so—[*he begins to adjust her robe so it falls off her shoulder*] and reassume the—

ARTEMISIA:
Papa.
Please do not touch her.

[*Her father's hand drops*—AGOSTINO *turns and looks at her*—MARIA *exits as the scene shifts.*]

10

ARTEMISIA [*to the audience*]:
Well, EXCUSE ME!
All right! All right! I didn't ask her!
I DON'T KNOW.
I'VE BARELY EVER EVEN TALKED TO OTHER GIRLS BEFORE.
And we have nothing in common, you know, she's—
Well, she *works*, and not just as a model.
Not that I am judging, but . . .
—and the men would never ask!
And she would never expect them to—
And I'm practically a man!
More like them than her anyhow.
Except better then these boys!
I feel that I am smarter—stronger—

(I was always proud)
I know that I can make my mark!
I sign my *Susanna and the Elders* in bold type—
Almost the only letters I know—
A-R-T-EMISIA!
And wait for the accolades to roll in!
And I, I, I . . . Wait.
And wait.
And wait.
For nothing.

While my *Susanna*—
Is noted on the marketplace for its oddity—
The—freakishness of its composition, and my own—
Freakishness, a 'woman painter'—
It is a bit as if a horse was taught to make hoofprints on canvas.
Nobody wants to buy
Art made by a beast of burden.
In fact, I am barely—if at all—
Credited. People think my father must
Have done it for me, or that—
I've simply traced over his lines
It is whispered about as a stunt, done by Orazio—
A way to hold on to his steadily decreasing popularity.

Papa says not to worry.

ORAZIO:
Sometimes the pieces don't sell, at first.

ARTEMISIA:
Papa says they will come around.

ORAZIO:
I tell you, patrons can be particular—

ARTEMISIA:
Papa is kind, gives me busywork

Doing ready-made pieces for lesser merchants
Who want something inoffensive to hang over their fireplace.

ORAZIO:
The markets tell us what they want!

ARTEMISIA:
Fruit, flowers, shells
Still lifes. Landscapes.
For a full year,
I paint and paint and paint
but
If you're not commissioned
It's a hobby
Not a trade.
My work is polite, pretty—unnoticed.
I watch the 'prentice boys advance and
Move on to assistant work
On the great murals, frescoes, masterpieces—
Some become independent right away.
Like Agostino Tassi.
Old enough and well connected enough to launch
Without any further training.
Worse—in 1610, my seventeenth year, he becomes a full guild member.
Worse still—he makes sure I know it.

11

[AGOSTINO *steps into the studio.* TUZIA *cleans, as* ARTEMISIA *paints a still life.*]

AGOSTINO:
Ah, Signora Gentileschi!! Always painting, painting, painting. Good for you! Flowers, eh? How lovely.

ARTEMISIA:

You're blocking my light, Signore.

AGOSTINO:

A thousand apologies. I don't know where my head is at—in composition, I suppose. [*He leans against her easel, as:*] Dunno if you've heard, but—I'm in serious consideration for a panel on the ceiling of Casa Buonarroti—a tribute to the great Michelangelo, depicting all his virtues, his genius, his—

ARTEMISIA:

I've heard.

AGOSTINO:

Ah! No doubt your father has been talking of it—it's quite a competition, you know, for this commission. I think he had hopes of being selected, but.

[*He shrugs.*]

ARTEMISIA:

Papa has plenty of commissions.

AGOSTINO:

Of course he does. But patrons sometimes want a break from the traditional, don't they? New blood.

[ARTEMISIA *ignores him. Micro-beat.*]

I myself have been asked to submit sketches on the theme of the Allegory of Inclination. Oh—that means—talent.

ARTEMISIA:

I know what it means.

AGOSTINO:

I'm feeling pretty good about it.

ARTEMISIA:

—Why are you even hanging about the studio now, Signore Tassi? You're no apprentice, anymore.

AGOSTINO:

No.

ARTEMISIA:

So—why don't you find your own space to—compose in.

AGOSTINO:

Your father invited me. Peers conversing with peers, you know.
Not that you would understand that—since you believe you have no peer.

ORAZIO:

Agostino! Come in, come in—have a cup of wine.

AGOSTINO:

Again—if you ever need any pointers.

ORAZIO:

Ah, Artemisia. Those flowers are coming along.

[*The men exit—* TUZIA *sidles up to* ARTEMISIA, *in a motherly fashion.*]

TUZIA:

You know, Artemisia—he's a good man, that Tassi. Que bello!
Coming up fast in the world.
And he seems—interested in you.

ARTEMISIA:

—I have no interest—in marrying.

TUZIA:

I said the same, once. But all women must have interest in such things—unless you intend to become a nun. [*She chuckles.*] And we do remember how well that went. [*Beat.*]
Your father will not always be here to protect you, child.

[*She reaches out to brush hair from* ARTEMISIA*'s forehead*—ARTEMISIA *shies away.*]

ARTEMISIA:
I'm making my own way.

TUZIA:
What, through painting flowers? You must accept the reality of this world, Misia. And if your mother were alive today, she would say the / same—

ARTEMISIA:
Tuzia! [*Icily*] Don't forget to empty the bin.

[TUZIA *exits, as* ARTEMISIA *fumes.*]

ARTEMISIA:
Can you even—
Fucking—
Talent!
Inclination!
Fucking Tassi, thought to be some—revolutionary—
Crowing about his victory over Papa—and the thought of my father
Always already so deferential, so carefully considerate—
Tipping his hat to that arrogant putan in the street—
Makes my hands shake and I cannot
do One! More! Brushstroke
Of one more fucking petal
On one more polite, pedestrian little still life! [*She throws the brush, angrily.*]
Talent!
Inclination!
Tassi!
When if they only could see—
What somebody else—

What I
Am capable of—
. . . .
. . . .
. . . .
Tuzia is right.
No, she is.
If I don't do something,
When my father is gone someday, I'll have—
Nothing.
Without a man—
For provision, protection, commission—
I cannot even hope to paint fruit
And be paid for it.
I think
I must, like Caravaggio,
The infamy, the criminal,
Do something so bold as to be un-ignorable
But what, but what, but—
. . . .
[*with thrilled nervousness and resolution*] Basta!

[*She carefully, swiftly repositions mirrors to reflect the stool—*]

So women have painted nudes before
And scarcely been remembered
So I have painted nudes before
And not been remarked
So I must dare bigger!

[*She grabs some of the flowers and fabric from the still life, sticks them in her hair, and begins disrobing, as:*]

The competition for this commission is fierce?
They want something revolutionary?
I'll show them an image of talent!

I'll show them a picture of inclination!
I'll show them I, I, I, Artemisia—

[*She sits and poses, draped only partially by the fabric.*]

And they will never forget it!!!!
If I must make something of myself
And all I have is my self—
I paint and paint and paint until—

[*A picture of Artemisia's* Allegory of Inclination *is projected—as* ORAZIO *enters, sees his mostly-naked daughter:*]

Artemisia Gentileschi, *Allegory of Inclination*, ca. 1615–17.
Oil on canvas. Courtesy of the Galleria in the Casa Buonarroti, Florence.

ORAZIO:
I—Santa Maria! Misia—

[ARTEMISIA *scrambles to cover herself*—ORAZIO *turns to the portrait.*]

Mi-si—

[ORAZIO *takes in the portrait, SCREAMS:*]

MISIA, WHAT HAVE YOU DONE!

12

ARTEMISIA:
I've made one hell of an impression, is what I've done!
Word of this gets around everywhere—phew, um, FAST
I'm a little disturbed by how many come to see it
And though my father briefly threatens to send me to the nunnery again
He cannot ignore the eyes of his peers—of the public!
You see—
Casa Buonnarti accepts my self-portrait!!!!
My talent, *my* inclination—
Prized above Agostino's, above anyone else's!
I've made my *name,* is what I've done!!!!
The aristocrats love a controversy
It's good for their conversation!
Scandal is profitable!
I made my name, is what I have done!
All Rome is abuzz! Though not all of it is pleased.

AGOSTINO [*screamingly angry, very fast*]:
La piccola cagna!!!! Mi ha rubato l'intero incarico: metteranno il suo pannello al posto del mio! A cosa sta arrivando questo mondo—quella puttana spudorata ladra!!!!

[*He spits and exits.*]

ARTEMISIA [*gleeful, speaking it*]:
—ha ha ha ha ha ha ha.

13

[ORAZIO *enters with wine; they are mid-drinking, celebratorily—* ARTEMISIA *serves her father.*]

ORAZIO:
Well, I cannot say—we do not have the eyes of the patrons now, my dear!
Not that I would have recommended such a—display—not that you asked!

ARTEMISIA [*smiling*]:
No.

ORAZIO:
No. But, one must be bold when one has the light! We will not lose this moment.
A little more wine, there?

ARTEMISIA [*she pours for him*]:
Is Agostino still running around town, cursing my name?

ORAZIO:
Noooo. Once he calmed down—he approached me, laughing. He knows it's all part of the game. Do promise me you'll be civil when you see him again, Misia!

ARTEMISIA [*easily*]:
I promise!

ORAZIO:
Good girl. You may be crossing paths with Tassi quite often, you know—for he and I are to collaborate!

ARTEMISIA:
Really.

ORAZIO:
Yes, a new commission! We will be doing the fresco of the Royal Saloon in the Quirinal Palace—can you believe it? And for an excellent sum, even if split! [*He drinks.*]

ARTEMISIA:
Papa—since it's my work that's gotten the attention—why don't you have me in, instead of Agostino?

ORAZIO:
Well, we must mend fences, my dear—besides, it's all about who the client finds exciting. And Agostino has excellent connections, you know.

ARTEMISIA:
Maybe I could join the two of you— / you could just ask—!

ORAZIO:
/ The deal is already struck, Misia. You will just—have to be content. /

ARTEMISIA:
/ But—

ORAZIO:
/ Besides.
Many believe women don't have the vision for a full ceiling.

[*Beat.*]

More wine, if you please.

14

ARTEMISIA:
Basta. So things are not perfect.

So I have to deal with that spaccone Agostino around the studio again—
Until their collaboration is finished.
But who cares? My bold move has paid off—
There is finally a commission for me, directly.
I've caught a benefactor's eye
In my own name.
I, I, I, Artemisia—
Am practically poised to enter the guild!
[*celebrating*] It's my first real professional piece for the poncy set.

And where should I start
This most important story
But at the very beginning?
I will repaint the *Madonna.*
The virgin on the wall.
But I won't make her like my dead mother, absent and remote.
I'll make her something . . . new.
My father trusts me, now, I know
To do right by the honor of his studio.
He even gives me
A little 'prentice boy of my own.
Matteo Favale.

[MATTEO *appears, uncomfortable in his own skin, pulling at his apprentice's homespun.*]

Poor thing. Just ten years old.
The smallest and the weakest of the boys
And probably the one with the least potential in the studio—
But still, he's *my* assistant, all the same!

MATTEO [*in despair*]:
But what should I even call you?!
Signore and Maestro don't work

ARTEMISIA:
He is ashamed of me, I think—

MATTEO:
—And Signora—that's just—awful—

ARTEMISIA:
The other boys are cruel to him—

MATTEO:
I'll feel as if I'm a ladies' maid—

ARTEMISIA:
Tease him for being my apprentice.

MATTEO:
—and so will all the others.

ARTEMISIA:
Signore should do fine, Matteo.

MATTEO:
But that doesn't—but you are a woman!

ARTEMISIA:
Only by technicality.

MATTEO:
If you say so—Signor-e.

ARTEMISIA:
But I will win him over with kindness, I will win him over by bits—
Strengthen him and build him up—
to be—as great as he can be!

MATTEO:
Signore, Signore, Signore—it just doesn't come off natural.

[ARTEMISIA *sits at her blank canvas—as* MATTEO *arranges the backdrop for a painting—*]

ARTEMISIA:
An apprentice, a commission
Even my own model—if she's only
Tuzia from upstairs,
Everything is going my way!
The story humming along,
The deadline soon to be met,
And I can feel the masterpiece will soon be within my reach, if
only—

15

[ORAZIO's *studio.* AGOSTINO, *once again, blocks* ARTEMISIA's *light.*]

AGOSTINO:
Signora Gentileschi.

ARTEMISIA:
This goddamned man will get out of my light!

AGOSTINO:
Buongiorno, Principessa.

ARTEMISIA:
Buongiorno, Signore Tassi. Could you please . . . scooch.

AGOSTINO:
Oh, of course. Don't mean to interfere.

ARTEMISIA:
Matteo, could you adjust the draping?

AGOSTINO:
Is your father home?

ARTEMISIA:
No, Signore. To the right, Matteo—more—further, there.

AGOSTINO:

Damnation. I was hoping he and I could sit and have a friendly cup or two of wine. Do you have any idea when he will come back?

ARTEMISIA:

Late, I think. He is out working on your much-vaunted fresco.

AGOSTINO:

I don't suppose you would like to have a cup or two, instead?

ARTEMISIA:

I am also working, Signore. And it is scarcely noon.
Matteo—will you fetch me some more crimson?

MATTEO:

Of course—Maestro, Signora—

ARTEMISIA:

Signore.

[AGOSTINO *laughs, again.*]

MATTEO:

Signore, Signore, Signore. It just doesn't sound quite right.

[MATTEO *leaves the room.* AGOSTINO *smirks and walks toward her.*]

AGOSTINO:

Well, *Signora* Gentileschi—

[TUZIA *enters, fully clothed. She stops when she sees* AGOSTINO—*who looks extremely annoyed to see her.*]

TUZIA:

Ah—Signore Tassi. [*Dropping a little curtsy*] Buongiorno, I did not know you were here.

[AGOSTINO *ignores her, examines a paintbrush—as* TUZIA *drifts toward the seat, her eyes still on him.*]

Artemisia—I am not sure—perhaps now is not the—correct time to sit.

ARTEMISIA:

Now is the only time, Tuzia. I've been prepping for over an hour.

TUZIA:

Only—I have many other things to do—and if you have company—

ARTEMISIA:

Don't be ridiculous. Sit.

[TUZIA *still hesitates.* ARTEMISIA, *exasperated:*]

Tuzia, we will lose the light!

[TUZIA, *uncomfortable, sits, fully clothed—and assumes the pose. Her eyes are still on* AGOSTINO. ARTEMISIA *starts working. Beat.*]

AGOSTINO:

What piece are you working on now, Madame?

ARTEMISIA:

Madonna and Child.

AGOSTINO:

D'you mind if I take a look?

ARTEMISIA:

Actually, I would rather you / not—

[AGOSTINO *whistles as he looks at the painting.*]

[*Behind us comes into view Artemisia Gentileschi's* Madonna and Child*—wherein the Virgin Mary breastfeeds the infant.*]

Artemisia Gentileschi, *Madonna and Child*, ca. 1613–14.
Oil on canvas. Courtesy of the Galleria Spada, Rome.

AGOSTINO:
Composing another scandal, I see.

ARTEMISIA:
She's feeding her child. That's what mothers do.

AGOSTINO:
Still. Bit . . . lewd, isn't it?

ARTEMISIA:
Lewd is in the eye of the beholder.

AGOSTINO:
Indeed. If I may give a thought—

[ARTEMISIA *sighs heavily.*]

The Virgin Mary—traditionally—is dressed in *blue.*
Cobalt pigment is expensive, I know, and perhaps you can't afford more than that bit in the corner. I could lend you some.

ARTEMISIA:
If I want it, my father will give it to me.

AGOSTINO:
Oh, I'm sure he will.
Or perhaps you could buy it for yourself. You're building quite a name—aren't you?

[TUZIA *shifts, uncomfortably.*]

ARTEMISIA:
Tuzia—do not move.

TUZIA:
My arms are getting tired.

AGOSTINO:
You know—it was a nasty trick
Stealing out that commission from under me.
Most men would be very angry.
But I am not most men.

TUZIA:
I want to get a glass of water.

ARTEMISIA:
Let me finish the robe, at least!

AGOSTINO:
I confess, you know—I liked your painting of Inclination.
Your self-portrait.

[TUZIA *has gotten up, fully.*]

ARTEMISIA:
Tuzia!

TUZIA:
I am very thirsty!!!

AGOSTINO:
Then Signora—you should get out of here.

[TUZIA *hesitates.*]

You heard me. Go!

ARTEMISIA:
Tuzia. Stay.

[TUZIA *begins to move toward the door.*]

TUZIA:
I don't want to stay here and argue.

ARTEMISIA [*VERY irritated*]:
Please.

TUZIA:
—I do not wish to get involved.

[*She slips out.* ARTEMISIA *is left alone with* AGOSTINO.]

16

[AGOSTINO *smiles upon* ARTEMISIA. *She is determined not to be intimidated.*]

AGOSTINO:
—I am a great admirer of your work, Signora Gentileschi.
—Artemisia.

[He leans close to her, obviously.
She processes this—then shies away, incredulous and half-amused.
She is a little weirded-out—a little taken aback—but not afraid.
She laughs, a little. It's awkward. It's even—a little bit—flattering. This is the first time she has ever been in this situation. She is not cognizant of being in any danger. She has lived and worked amongst men all her life, under the unspoken protection of her father.
And she is only eighteen.]

I don't mean to make you uncomfortable, Signora.
But I don't think you are uncomfortable often—are you?

ARTEMISIA [*incredulous, still almost amused*]:
Signore Tassi—

AGOSTINO:
I suppose that's part of the thrill—
Being stared at, being observed.
Why do you display yourself if you don't like it.

ARTEMISIA:
—my father will be home any minute.

AGOSTINO:
You said he would be out late.

[*He comes toward her.*]

ARTEMISIA:
Signore—

AGOSTINO:
I do not know why we cannot be friends.

ARTEMISIA [*still not afraid*]:
I'm afraid— you have to leave, Signore.
[*not really trying to sell it*] I do not feel well, at all—I think I have a fever.

AGOSTINO:
It is I who have the fever.

[*He tries to kiss her.*]

ARTEMISIA [*trying to minimize it, almost smiling*]:
Stop—

[*He tries again. Now she is not smiling, at all.*]

Stop.
[*He comes in again. She slaps him.*] I said stop! [*He catches her wrist*]—no!

[*He grabs her—she begins to scream, and he muffles her.*]

[*A frozen beat. She steps out of the scene.*]

17

ARTEMISIA:

I do not want to tell this part of the story.
Not again.
Must we tell this?

[*Beat. Perhaps, as she speaks, behind her flash images—dozens, of all the many depictions of the* Rape of the Sabine Women. *Stylized violence depicted beautifully—the subject of so much art. Perhaps as she talks, she slowly tears her clothes, like a woman in mourning. We do not see the assault. All we have is her word.*]

ARTEMISIA:

I have always thought I was as smart, as strong—
As any of the men around me.
But now I learn what it is to be—smaller.
He pushes me into—
Not my room, but—
My father's room.
My father's own bed.
I am fighting as hard as I can, I scratch and slap
And he is—*smiling*.
My hardest struggle is a joke to him.
I try to scream and then—
He covers my mouth so entirely,
Shoves fabric within it—
That it is a struggle just to breathe.
His hand is on my throat—
When his weight is on me, he is so heavy—
And he presses harder and harder down as I struggle,
And I feel a burning—
And I think that—I think that if I keep fighting—
I think that I will die.

And I want to live.
And so to live—
I stop fighting.
I freeze.
I leave my body
My body, God's creation.
I do not want to stay there while he—
On my father's ceiling, there is a long crack
An old chink in the plaster and I
Stare at it now, as he.
A spider is weaving a web in the crack.
As it is happening,
I wish myself
Out of my_self
And into the body of that spider,
Hidden away in the shadows.
Weaving her web in peace.
I picture it as hard as I can
So I may not feel it—
While he.
I wish myself anything and anywhere other than
I, I, I.
Until it is done.

[*Any images behind her fade.*]

He rolls off.
He is still *smiling.*
He is not bothered at all.

I do not know how I got to the knife
My father had left by his bed.
But I must not be moving fast
Not very fast because Agostino is still
Almost laughing—as I grab it

My voice—it's like a nightmare
When you try to scream but cannot—
I feel so—

ARTEMISIA:

[*This is completely inaudible to us.*]

I could kill you.

AGOSTINO:
What was that?
Hm?

[*He looks at the knife she is holding. He laughs a little.*]

ARTEMISIA:
But I am not a heroine of some old story.
I cannot hold the knife.
My hands are shaking too badly
And I do not have the strength.

[ARTEMISIA *drops the knife. Sits.*]

AGOSTINO:
Please don't be so dramatic.
A little blood, all maids go through it. And all women suffer a bit,
when they learn this act.
I've suffered, for love of you!

[*He reaches out to her—she backs away. He drops his hand, tsks.*]

I will make it right, my sweetheart.
I will marry you.

[*She backs away, shakes her head.*]

ARTEMISIA:
I will tell—

AGOSTINO [*putting his clothes back on*]:
Who? Your father?
I wouldn't.
It would be the ruin of you—
Worse, it would be the ruin of Orazio.
The end of his work.
The end of your work.
Besides—you wanted it.

ARTEMISIA:
I didn't—

AGOSTINO:
You *did.* You still do.
And Tuzia will swear the same.

ARTEMISIA:
/ She—

AGOSTINO:
/ She needed the money—and I am becoming a wealthy man.

[*He arranges himself in a mirror, carefully hides a scratch mark. As he does:*]

I have a real future ahead of me. If you are my wife, I will shepherd your career—introduce you to the best patrons, make you an even greater force than you are. If you will treat me as your husband, my love, you can gain—so much.
Why lose your virtue for nothing?

ARTEMISIA:
No.

AGOSTINO [*he drops his hand*]:
You've always been a smart girl, Artemisia.

Make smart choices now.
You don't want to break your father's heart.

[He exits.
A moment. Two. Three.
She gets up—slowly gathers herself, leaves. She is hurting.]

[*After a moment. The little boy,* MATTEO, *steps out—his eyes wide—his hands are shaking. He drops the red pigment all over the floor.*]

18

[MATTEO *exits—red pigment all over the floor—as Artemisia comes in and strips the bed. She uses the sheets to wipe up the red pigment—staining them—as she speaks to the audience.*]

ARTEMISIA:
Rome is a city of ancient mores and rules, and one rule
Has been very clear since Octavian,
—since before those old Bible stories—
If a woman loses her maidenhead outside of marriage,
Her honor is lost, too.
If her honor is lost,
So is her father's—her whole
Household's, they will be ruined.

And if I should accuse Agostino
And nobody should believe me—
And why should they ever believe me?
Me who paints myself naked
Me who was raised by no mother, thrown out of a nunnery
Me who lives and works amongst the men—
Then I can be whipped through the streets as a whore
Or have my tongue slit as a gossip
Or be stoned, by my neighbors, as a blasphemer.

Not ten years ago the law with the blessing of the Pope himself
Tortured on the rack and beheaded a woman, Beatrice Cenci—for taking arms against
Her rapist—though he was her own father.
And she was a noblewoman! And a paragon of virtue, they all say—
And so—if they would do that to her . . . ?

There is no—benefit to telling the truth,
Except acknowledging the truth
Of my body.
But if I can—
If I can forget that—
If he will marry me,
My wrong would be undone in the eyes of the church, the law.
I will save my father, my work, my—self.

Why should I suffer for nothing?!
If I cannot undo it
—and I cannot undo it . . .
I can make it right.
I can control it.
And so, at eighteen years old—
I submit.
I choose, if this is a choice.
I consent, if this is consenting.
I become Agostino Tassi's mistress.

ACT 2

1

[The same studio. ARTEMISIA *stands in the same position as at the end of act 1, by the bed.* AGOSTINO *reenters;* TUZIA *shows him in. He is smiling.* TUZIA *exits.]*

ARTEMISIA:

For months, Agostino and I meet—
Whenever my father is out.
Tuzia opens the door to him,
And turns her face away.
It's this or I lose everything—
I lose control of what happened.
And so I finally do as I was told—
—I compromise.
I compromise my self.

I bleed at first, and then it stops.
It doesn't always even hurt the same way—
But then, I have stopped fighting.
He teaches me all the tricks he prefers.
I give him just what his body wants.

And every time I do I leave my own body further—
Perhaps my body is his body, now, as he says,
And this is what it means to become one flesh.

AGOSTINO:
Do you like that?
Do you like that?

ARTEMISIA:
Did I ever take pleasure in it?
In pleasing him?
Did I—
I, I.

AGOSTINO:
Good girl.

ARTEMISIA:
I try to forget.

AGOSTINO:
Good girl.

ARTEMISIA:
He says that he is only waiting
For the right moment to ask my father for my hand.
After they finish their fresco, together.
Papa will skewer him on the dowry otherwise, he says.
He doesn't want to mix business and pleasure, he says.
Did I ever take pleasure in—?

AGOSTINO:
Good girl.

ARTEMISIA [*banishing him*]:
Basta!

[*He exits, smiling.*]

ARTEMISIA:

Perhaps he is right, perhaps all women always feel like this.
He is the first kiss I ever have, the first naked man I ever see.
—Even in marriage, nobody talks about
What happens behind bedroom doors.
This may be normal.
And I *want* it to be *so* normal—I want to go right back to the person I was—
—before the thing I don't want to remember—
Happened to—someone else.

I finish my *Madonna*.

And I do not use blue on her, ever.

After my *Madonna*, I tell my father—
I need time to think—
To plan my next piece.
But I struggle with my vision.
I sketch, I throw things out.
I cannot decide what to do.
My senses are all—
I am a terrible mentor to Matteo, he arranges and rearranges dry brushes,
Unused pigments, clean palettes, always watching my face—
Anxious to know what I am thinking.
When I will start creating again.
But whenever I look at the blank canvas—
I do not know where to begin, cannot quite—(focus).

I stop eating, much.
Agostino says he likes me skinny.
Then I start eating more and more.
I try to make myself—
Untouchable, but Tassi does not stop touching.

My father does not notice.
He is consumed with the fresco they are co-creating.

2

[ARTEMISIA *and* ORAZIO *sit down to eat—bread and oil and water.*]

ORAZIO:
I really think this is it, Misia. This could be the one that cements my reputation.

ARTEMISIA:
Yes, Papa.

[*She eats.*]

ORAZIO:
I'll need Cosimo to come appraise it, of course, give his expert eye—d'you remember all those years ago, when he took you to task on the Caravaggio?

ARTEMISIA:
Yes, Papa.

[*She eats.*]

ORAZIO:
But I think he'll be impressed by this one. Tasteful, of course—but a real—real step forward from my usual work. I owe so much of it to Agostino.

ARTEMISIA:
Pass the oil, Papa.

[ARTEMISIA *eats and eats, as:*]

ORAZIO:
He is—quite a valuable collaborator, you know.
He excels at the trompe l'oeil, in particular—has a real knack for it.
You really should take some lessons from him, my love.
He always offers such valuable perspect—

[*Surprised*]

Misia—have you eaten all the bread?

ARTEMISIA:
. . . Pardon me, Papa. I am feeling sick.

[*She leaves the table—*ORAZIO *stares after her.*]

3

ARTEMISIA:

[*She sits in front of a canvas—it's blank.*]

For months, I keep trying to restart—
But I never quite raise paint to canvas.
I question myself in every moment—
The lines never quite solidify.
I feel . . . lost.

And whatever Agostino is, he certainly
Wants to give me direction.

[AGOSTINO *enters.*]

AGOSTINO:
You're my muse

ARTEMISIA:
—he says

AGOSTINO:
You're my inspiration

ARTEMISIA:
At times that seems like . . . something.

[*She lies next to* AGOSTINO, *removes some of her clothes.*]

One day, in the studio—after he's finished—he rolls off and says—

AGOSTINO:
Let me paint you into a panel of the fresco.

ARTEMISIA
The one you are doing with Papa?

AGOSTINO:
Why not?
Let me capture you, just as you are. Let me give you—immortality.

[*He touches her face.*]

I'll sketch it now.

ARTEMISIA:
Papa could be home, any moment.

AGOSTINO:
No, he'll be out late. His work on the fresco . . . is not going well.

ARTEMISIA:
What?

AGOSTINO:
Too conventional. Again. Not an imaginative thinker, our simple Orazio. I've been propping him up, but I think, deep down inside, he knows how badly he is fail / ing

ARTEMISIA:
/ Don't you ever speak badly about my father!

AGOSTINO:
Come on, now, don't get so /

ARTEMISIA:
/ —I mean it.

[*She begins pulling on her clothes.*]

I should get dressed.

AGOSTINO:
No. Not yet.
Come, just let me make a sketch. I want to catch you—just like this.

ARTEMISIA:
I don't want to.

AGOSTINO:
Artemisia. [*A bit of a threat*] Do not give me trouble.

ARTEMISIA:
[*To the audience*] I don't want to end up with nothing.
[*To him, doing a good cover*] You will have no more trouble from me.
One sketch. Quickly.

AGOSTINO:
Excellent. Don't move.

ARTEMISIA:
Perhaps this is my destiny.

AGOSTINO:
Look at you—set just as I like.

[AGOSTINO *begins arranging her—slipping her dress off her shoulder. She does not resist.*]

It's not so hard, is it?

[*Behind her, starts to flicker the projection of the panel which is thought to depict the portrait of Artemisia Gentileschi at the Quirinal Palace.*]

ARTEMISIA:
Maybe things will be different once we're married.
Maybe I'll have his babies and learn to love them.
Maybe I'll forget—how it all started.

[AGOSTINO *sketches as the panel comes more and more into view.*]

AGOSTINO:
Loosen up. Jesu, you're so tight. And not only in the good way.

ARTEMISIA:
My stupid body knows the truth—

AGOSTINO:
Not quite a professional, hm?

ARTEMISIA:
My body tenses every time he's near.
But if I can never be safe
And I can never be whole again—

AGOSTINO [*very annoyed*]:
Close your eyes, if that helps.

[ARTEMISIA *closes her eyes.*]

ARTEMISIA:
There must have been women who survived like this before.
Maybe I can make myself—be happy.

[*Unseen by either* AGOSTINO, *who is sketching, or* ARTEMISIA, ORAZIO *has entered.*]

Maybe—maybe—mayb—

ORAZIO:
Artemisia.

[*Her eyes fly open.*]

What are you doing?!

[*She scrambles to pull her dress fully on. Beat.*]

ARTEMISIA:
Papa . . .

AGOSTINO:
Now, Orazio, it's not what it looks like—

ORAZIO:
What is it, then?! Eh?! EH?!

AGOSTINO:
Calm down, old man—

ORAZIO:
Bastardo! Mostro!! [*He shoves* AGOSTINO.] You disrespect me in this way—my daughter! In my own—! While I complete our work!

AGOSTINO:
Whoa, whoa—you don't understand the situation— / Have Artemisia explain to you—

ORAZIO:
/ I understand well enough! Out now! Out! OUT BEFORE I KILL YOU!

AGOSTINO:
Be careful what you say, Orazio. I am not a good man to cross.
Talk to your daughter.

[AGOSTINO *exits. Beat.*]

ARTEMISIA:
Papa, I—

ORAZIO:
Misia—why? Why would you put yourself in such a position?!!!!

ARTEMISIA:
I didn't!

[*Beat.* ORAZIO *starts advancing on her. She backs up.*]

ORAZIO:
. . . How long has this been going on?!
What, beneath my nose, you—you what, betray me, seduce him, you laugh at me, your foolish father, with no—no sight—to see you mock me in my own studio—where I taught you, where I have trusted you to uphold my legacy—

ARTEMISIA:
STOP! I did NOT betray you!! Or, or seduce him—and—but it doesn't matter—
You won't be ruined, we won't be—
He has promised to marry me!
And I will still paint, he will help you, me, and—
And I can live with it, being his [*it's hard to get the word out*] *wife*—and everything will be fine!!!!

ORAZIO:
Oh, Misia—Misia—you are a fool. And I am one, too, to let that man into my home—

ARTEMISIA:
—Papa—

ORAZIO:
Artemisia. Agostino is already married.

4

ARTEMISIA:
Married.
He has a wife in Naples.
The boys all knew—the boys always know.
Even if they do not speak of it to me.
Though he and his wife do not live together.
He is no less bound in the eyes of the church.

And so I compromised for nothing, again and again.

I tell my father—everything.
What use is hiding the truth now?
And he is my God, and I want—
Absolution for my shame.

Papa, to his credit, believes me—he curses Agostino
As a villain, a criminal.
Papa is determined to find justice.
He's a traditionalist.
A man of faith.
Rome is a city of angels and devils
A place of old mores and rules
And this is not the first time rules have been broken.
And so—without asking my opinion on the matter—
Papa decides to test the strength of our honor before the public.
And the gallery is full—
When he brings this matter to the courts.

5

[The courtroom—a high table, chairs. An unseen gallery full of people watch. Sounds of the crowd. They whisper and talk as ARTEMISIA *enters the scene. A* JUDGE *sits—he's a nobleman, in rich black robes. He believes, very much, that he is a modern man; a progressive. He may actually be one.]*

JUDGE:

Silence, silence!

[*The murmuring stops—the* JUDGE *arranges some papers.*]

Before us, dear people
Stands one Orazio Gentileschi
And one Agostino Tassi.
Signore Gentileschi accuses Signore Tassi of the violent disgrace of his maiden daughter, one Artemisia Gentileschi—
And also of the theft of a certain painting on the subject of Judith and Holofernes—
Valued at three hundred ducats.

[*The men jump right in, at full explosiveness, à la Kavanaugh.*]

AGOSTINO:

Your Honor—!

ARTEMISIA:

Evidently Agostino was skulking around the studio

ORAZIO:

Your Honor—!

ARTEMISIA:

For more than one reason.

AGOSTINO:

That painting was mine! / You old fool, you wouldn't know good art if it bit you on the ass /

ORAZIO:

/ Even a casual appraisal of said painting—will prove that this man is a thief / and if he is capable of such, does it not follow that he would do worse!

AGOSTINO:

/ I'll sue you for slander, Orazio, I'll own your whole studio before I'm through!

JUDGE:

/ One at a time, gentleman! One at a time!

ORAZIO:

—call in the experts, Your Honor, call them in at once!

JUDGE:

Rest assured, Signore, experts have been consulted. Now—to the first charge. Signore Gentileschi—it is your attestation that your maiden daughter was deflowered by this man?

ORAZIO:

Your Honor, my wrongs know no end. As of two years ago, sir, Agostino Tassi and I were joined in close friendship. Not only did I love him, but also—when he was compromised for having carnal relations with his own sister-in law—

ARTEMISIA:

Wait

ORAZIO:

I used powerful connections to save him

ARTEMISIA:

What

ORAZIO:

Then I arranged to paint the fresco in the Quirinal Palace with this man, for which Agostino alone was celebrated—

ARTEMISIA:

My father knew.

ORAZIO:

—and to reward me for my advocacy, he by force and threats dared to have his way with my daughter!

ARTEMISIA:

That Agostino was no saint—

JUDGE:
/ Signore—

ORAZIO:
/ Then, he stoked my daughter's hopes that he would marry—

ARTEMISIA:
Why didn't he warn me

ORAZIO:
And also introduce her to patrons—and a thousand such other lies—

ARTEMISIA:
Why did he ever protect him?

JUDGE:
/ Signore—

ORAZIO:
/ Until the news reached my daughter's ears that he was married already—and it was confirmed that this scoundrel had killed her with / false promises—

JUDGE:
/ Signore

ORAZIO:
I beg you to demonstrate before all of Rome, Your Honor—that justice shall be served, no matter the connections of the accused—that all men should know what crime was done to me in the name of friendship!

ARTEMISIA:
Why were they ever friends.

AGOSTINO:
Your Honor, I have letters—attesting to my character, from many high-placed within various courts, from bishops as well as gentry. / I have outstanding commissions with some of / the—

ORAZIO:

/ As I say, he is connected, he is well connected, and will boast of it / at every

JUDGE:

/ Signori—

AGOSTINO:

And he may say what he will, but I can produce a hundred testimonies, to the contrary, on every account, and will do so / whenever you

ORAZIO:

Yes, I am sure you have many skilled liars in your circles! / Va' in malora!

JUDGE:

/ Gentlemen! Please!!!!!
Signore Tassi—testimonies shall indeed be collected, in due time.
Is it your estimation, Signore Gentileschi—that your daughter is in good health?

ORAZIO:

She is—was, generally, yes—before this man destroyed her!

JUDGE:

And she is of sound mind?

ORAZIO:

Of course.

JUDGE:

Then do sit, in the public gallery.
Signora Gentileschi must answer for the first charge.

ORAZIO:

But—but this is my case. I thought—that I should advocate for her!

JUDGE:

We are in the new century, Signore, and the law does try to keep up with the times. The women must be heard.

ORAZIO:

Sir—

JUDGE:

It is understandable that a father would want to believe that his daughter did not choose dishonor. But we must have the girl, without any external pressure.

ORAZIO:

But—she is young, and easily led, as you can see, and is not capable of . . . !

JUDGE [*holding up a hand*]:

Signora?

ARTEMISIA:

I am—capable, Your Honor.

JUDGE:

Signore, you may yet be asked to elaborate on the particulars of the allegedly stolen painting. Sit, and be silent until called upon.

[ORAZIO *stares at* ARTEMISIA *and exits, however unwillingly. He sits in the public gallery—which is our audience.*]

JUDGE:

Now, Signora. Let it be known that this trial
Will leave no private matter unexamined.
What's more—the penalties for perjury are harsh.
You may be imprisoned, or flogged—or even worse—
If we find you have accused an innocent man.
And so—it must be your choice.
Do you still wish to proceed, Signora Gentileschi?

[ARTEMISIA *balks. Beat.*]

Do you still wish to—

ARTEMISIA:
I wish—to have the truth known.

JUDGE:
Good. [*He nods, then:*] Then let us start with the uncomfortable facts. The midwives whom we sent to examine you have informed this court—that you are no maid.

ARTEMISIA:
I could have told you that, sir.

AGOSTINO:
But I was not the one who deflowered her!

JUDGE:
Who else but you?

AGOSTINO:
It could be any one of—dozens, from what I hear.

ARTEMISIA:
/ No—there were / never any (other!)

AGOSTINO:
/ But I will not name them! I, for one, will not stoop to accusation of an innocent man!

ARTEMISIA:
I have never had relations with anyone but Signore Tassi!

JUDGE:
By your own consent?

ARTEMISIA:
. . . Not the first time, no! And after . . .
I was promised that he would marry me, sir—

AGOSTINO:
/ Your—

ARTEMISIA:

/ And to save my honor—I agreed to—lie with him again, and again! But only because I was deceived!

JUDGE:

Mm. You do not live with your wife, Signore Tassi?

AGOSTINO:

No, sir. She is a bitter woman—and full of delusions and jealousies. As you have heard, she accused me of having relations with my sister-in-law—a claim which, I will point out, I have never been found guilty of, in any court.

JUDGE:

Do you confess that you had relations with Artemisia Gentileschi?

AGOSTINO:

I am a man, as God made me—and weak.
When she made clear that I was very welcome—

ARTEMISIA:

No, no— / that's not true—

AGOSTINO:

/ I was unfaithful to my wife, I do confess it! Shall I be cast out of society, for this common sin?

JUDGE:

Did you promise to marry her?

AGOSTINO:

I said many foolish things, in love-talk.

ARTEMISIA:

"Love-talk!" It was as good as a contract!

AGOSTINO:

Everybody knew that I was married. She heard what she wanted to hear.

ARTEMISIA:
I never wanted—any of it!

AGOSTINO:
You *did. You know you did.*
But I do not ask you to rely only on what I say, Your Honor. I call, for my defense—Tuzia Medaglia.

[TUZIA, *dressed with extreme care and modesty, comes into the courtroom.* ARTEMISIA *stares at her as she does*—TUZIA, *unerringly, sits at the front of the room.*]

JUDGE:
Signora Medaglia, do you swear to tell only God's holy truth in this room?

TUZIA [*crossing herself*—AGOSTINO *follows suit*]:
I hope I always may fear God, sir. I do.

JUDGE:
And do you know this woman?

TUZIA:
Indeed—I have known her since she was a child. I live in quarters above her father's studio on Via Della Croce. And for a small reduction in my rent, Signore Gentileschi would often task me—to wash their linens, and clean, and watch his daughter, and all that. And I am sad to say—

JUDGE:
Yes—

TUZIA:
—I regret to say that she was always a prideful girl. She often stuck her head out upon the street, to watch the youths below. Traveled all about the city—mixed freely amongst the boys in her father's studio. And once—she was expelled from a nunnery. We never did find out for what!

JUDGE:

—do you know anything of her relationship with this man?

TUZIA:

Oh, it appeared to me a friendly one, sir. He visited her often, alone—and they would close the doors upon the room. I can say no more.

JUDGE:

You condoned this behavior?

TUZIA:

I am not her mother, Your Honor—and she always made it very clear, that she did not want me to treat her as such. [*She sniffs.*]

ARTEMISIA:

And were you ever given money by Signore Tassi, Tuzia?!

AGOSTINO:

Is she allowed to ask questions?!

ARTEMISIA:

Were you paid to leave me alone with him?!!!

TUZIA:

—Your Honor, I did in fact take some small change from this fellow to visit upon this signora. Perhaps it is not—the most proper thing, but I am a poor widow, with very little to fall back upon—and my rent was too goddamned high.

JUDGE:

Language, Signora.

TUZIA:

Mi scusi.

ARTEMISIA:

And what about the first time, Tuzia? Do you know what happened then?

TUZIA:
I was not there, Your Honor—

ARTEMISIA:
You were just outside the doors—

TUZIA:
How can I say what transpired?

ARTEMISIA:
Didn't I ask you not to go?! And did you hear the struggle—did you hear me trying to scream?
Did you see the sheets, in the laundry after?
. . . Tuzia. You have known me—since I was a little girl.

[*Beat.*]

TUZIA:
Your Honor, it is my true impression—that Artemisia was always excited to see him.

ARTEMISIA:
/ Liar!

TUZIA:
/ She was glad enough for the flirtation, she had no other suitors! Brazen, she was, thought herself much better than me, than any other woman—that was what brought her to ruin!

ARTEMISIA:
There! There, you see, Your Honor—she says that I had no other suitors. How can I have lost my honor to dozens of men, as Signore Tassi says—if she only ever saw one.

AGOSTINO:
Surely the point is made! This woman says Signora Gentileschi welcomed me in, time and time again—whether or not she saw

other lovers, does not disprove their existence. The case should be dismissed.

ARTEMISIA:
He has paid / her!

JUDGE:
/ We will hear other opinions on this matter!
Signora Megdalia—you will wait outside, until you are summoned to answer for your testimony.

TUZIA:
"Answer"? Your Honor, how may I answer?!!

JUDGE:
You will wait under guard. Deputy?

[*A* DEPUTY *appears and starts escorting* TUZIA *outside, roughly; as he does, she starts shouting, desperately.*]

TUZIA:
I have only told the truth of—what I saw! I did not want to get involved! [*She struggles.*] No! I do not want to get involved!

[TUZIA *is escorted out. Beat.*]

AGOSTINO:
As to my next witness—

JUDGE:
Peace, Signore Tassi. Not every witness shall be in your employ. Orazio Gentileschi has also provided names. Next, we shall hear a letter—volunteered from one Cosimo Quorli—recently made Papal Steward.

ARTEMISIA [*jubilantly*]:
Cosimo—Cosimo, my father's friend!

JUDGE:

Signore Quorli has graciously agreed to give his opinion on the provenance of the painting in question, as well as his knowledge of the parties involved.

ARTEMISIA:

—Cosimo—who taught me how to swear!

JUDGE:

I will read it aloud.
"Honorable assembly—

[*The* DEPUTY *appears again, but as* COSIMO*—outside the reality of the courtroom, via the letter*:]

JUDGE [*simultaneous with* COSIMO]: "I am called upon by the court to give my opinion of this matter, / as a practiced appraiser of art. But I will disclose my prejudices— [*The* JUDGE*'s voice fades out.*]

COSIMO [*simultaneous with the* JUDGE]: /—as a practiced appraiser of art. But I will disclose my prejudices, that no man may call me unjust. I have been friends with Orazio Gentileschi since we were apprentices, and respect his work. I knew Agostino Tassi only through our guild, and thought his arrogance often outpaced his artistry. I only met Signora Gentileschi once—and while I found her a curious little thing—have never troubled myself about her since. But—

ARTEMISIA:

He has not seen me since—

COSIMO:

"While I do not have much personal knowledge of Artemisia Gentileschi, Your Honor, I have heard many tales of her over the years."

ARTEMISIA:
Since—

COSIMO:
"Since her youth, she was given free reign in her father's studio, and allowed to mingle in and out of male company, and she has suffered every consequence that would be expected."

ARTEMISIA:
I was a *child*.

COSIMO:
"There is a stonecutter who works in her father's house, with whom you could not even trust a female cat, and he says he has known her parts intimately, and will describe them to you in excruciating detail, when bought even a single cup of wine."

ARTEMISIA:
Another of my father's *friends*!

COSIMO:
"The apprentice boys all boasted of her favors, since before she was able to bleed—"

ARTEMISIA:
I'm sure he's telling the truth.

COSIMO:
"although they say she is careful not to get with child, and practices a wide range of whore's tricks to do so."

ARTEMISIA:
I'm sure they do all say these things—

COSIMO:
"But this is not the worst of the tales. As you know, Signora Gentileschi gained her fame from a rather shocking self-portrait. I am told that she did not paint said work at all, but that it was

the work of Orazio. They say she has posed nude for her own father . . . and maybe even worse."

ARTEMISIA:
How did I never think—how they'd laugh behind my back?

COSIMO:
"And while I do not wish to think such of my old friend, I do believe that every painting done 'by' Artemisia Gentileschi may be an effort to gain attention by Orazio, who is habitually—and perhaps unfairly—overlooked by clients and peers alike."

ARTEMISIA:
How did I never see—

COSIMO:
"Only a master could have created these works. And Artemisia Gentileschi, by her nature, cannot be a master."

ARTEMISIA:
—how much they all despised me?

COSIMO:
"And to show my fairhandedness—I will say that the painting theoretically stolen by Agostino Tassi appears to be not of his mark, and that said claim may indeed be valid."
"Your humble vassal and servant— / Cosimo Quorli.

JUDGE: / vassal and servant—Cosimo Quorli.

[COSIMO/DEPUTY *disappears. The* JUDGE *puts down the letter as* AGOSTINO *steps in*—]

AGOSTINO:
Your Honor, while I thank God for this man's honest appraisal of character, I will not and cannot admit—that the painting was ever /

JUDGE:

/ Hold your tongue, sir—and we shall return to said painting! Signora Gentileschi. How do you answer this letter?

ARTEMISIA:

My work is my own.

JUDGE:

That—is not the central accusation. I am surprised you do not defend your reputation!

ARTEMISIA:

Cosimo Quorli shares only disgusting, idle gossip, as we may hear of any virtuous person in the city!

JUDGE:

Virtuous people, Signora, do not often find themselves in such compromising positions.

ARTEMISIA:

I have only had relations with one man—this man—and I tell you I did not choose it!

JUDGE:

You said you did not choose it the *first* time.

ARTEMISIA:

—Yes. I mean—no, I did not.

JUDGE:

You claimed it was by force. And were you a maid when this happened?

ARTEMISIA:

Yes.

JUDGE:

And did you bleed?

ARTEMISIA:

—Yes.

JUDGE:

And yet you did consent the second time? [*She nods.*] And was it always painful?

ARTEMISIA:

(Not as)—the first time I had fought him, and then—

JUDGE:

And then you never fought him again?
Did you ever say no, or ever again refuse him?
Did you make clear, to this Signore, that you did not enjoy his continued advances?

ARTEMISIA:

I did not feel that—I could

JUDGE:

—And did you ever take pleasure in said submission?

ARTEMISIA:

Excuse me?

JUDGE:

Did you ever receive enjoyment, from any of his acts?

ARTEMISIA:

—sir, my father is watching.

JUDGE:

We said we would unearth private matters, Signora. Did you ever take pleasure in /

ARTEMISIA:

/ I

JUDGE:

—did you ever take pleasure in the act, / Signora?

ARTEMISIA:
/ I—

JUDGE:
Did you / ever—

ARTEMISIA:
/ I have now related all that happened, Your Honor!!!!! Between Agostino and myself.

[*Beat.*]

AGOSTINO:
She may regret her lost honor, Signore, and fear her father's anger, but she welcomed me, into her bed, laughing, a hundred times.
And she has not a shred of evidence to the contrary!

ARTEMISIA:
I myself am the proof, my word, me—I, I, I!

[*Beat.*]

JUDGE:
Well said.

AGOSTINO:
Your Honor—!

JUDGE:
HUSH, sir. I WILL LET YOU KNOW WHEN YOU MAY SPEAK AGAIN.

[AGOSTINO *almost retorts—then thinks better of it, and sits.*]

. . . Signora Gentileschi. I wish you to know that your voice is heard in this room. I do agree that some of the evidence given against you is flawed. And if your word is your own best proof—then I must offer you a way to strengthen your statement, in the eyes of all here. An examination.

ARTEMISIA:
(An—?) I have already had the midwives—

JUDGE:
Not that. A simple physical—test.

ARTEMISIA:
What do you mean?

[*The* DEPUTY *has brought out the sibille—a torture device—cords of rope which are tied around a person's hands, which are then tightened, terribly.* ARTEMISIA *stares at them.*]

JUDGE:
Le sibille. A device for the hands.
Without this examination, I cannot see
How we can give your testimony its due weight.
And it will all be done publicly, so that nobody may say this court participates in the miscarriage of justice that so often occurs behind closed doors.
Do not worry, Signora. It should not cause—permanent damage.

ARTEMISIA [*to the audience, wildly*]:
Papa.
I am a child again, I think
Papa—Papa, I look out to the gallery, try to find his face—
Surely he will shout out against this!
But he is lost in the crowd
And he does not speak.
And I—

JUDGE:
Signora. Will you take the test.

DEPUTY:
We'll need your hands, Signora.

ARTEMISIA:
—my hands are how I do my work—

JUDGE:
Do you value your craft more than your honor?

ARTEMISIA:
—I cannot work *without* my reputation.

JUDGE:
The more reason to submit!

ARTEMISIA:
Agostino is the criminal, not me!

JUDGE:
Yours is the complaint, yours the accusation—and we have heard many damning testimonies about your character. You have more against you than with you, Signora. [*Beat.*]
—It is your choice, in the end.
And so—do you consent?

[ARTEMISIA *hesitates—one beat, two—*]

ARTEMISIA:
—I don't want to come away with nothing.

[*She nods. The* DEPUTY *begins to put the sibille upon her—*]

This is the ring you have given me, Tassi, and these your promises.

JUDGE:
Proceed.

[*The* DEPUTY *fastens the sibille as she speaks.*]

ARTEMISIA:
It looks like a child's game
As they fasten the cords around my fingers, tight.
Like cat's cradle, as I saw the other girls play in the nunnery
All those years ago. So simple.
Delicate even.
A lady's torture, for a lady's trial.
They fasten the strings
And—

[*She steps out of the story.*]

I don't want to tell this part of the story—
Do we have to tell this?

[*Beat. The* DEPUTY *starts tightening.*]

And.
They start slow, at first.

JUDGE:
Is it true Artemisia Gentileschi?

ARTEMISIA:
Then they tighten and tighten
And the pressure builds and builds

JUDGE:
Is it true Signora

ARTEMISIA:
And you can't imagine when it starts to cut—the pain, every nerve

JUDGE:
You can make this go away

ARTEMISIA:
Is screaming burning all you can feel is the slicing down to the bone
And you'll do anything to get away anything—anything to make it stop—stop—

[*She snaps back into the story, being cut—*]

stop STOP

JUDGE:
IS IT TRUE, ARTEMISIA GENTILESCHI

ARTEMISIA [*back in the scene*]:
IT IS TRUE IT IS TRUE IT IS ALL TRUE.

[*The* DEPUTY *pauses. She sobs.*]

Please, please, stop. Please. Please.

JUDGE:
You may release her.

[ARTEMISIA *collapses, holding her maimed hands to her body.*]

ARTEMISIA:
Oh God, oh God, oh my God.

[*She cries. Long beat.*]

JUDGE:
And so, Signore Tassi?

AGOSTINO:
Your Honor, of course she has no choice but to commit! This is no proof at all, that she is not lying!

JUDGE:
I *profoundly* disagree.
Such reactions cannot be false, Signore.
It is why the state, and the church
Gives us such valuable tools.

[*To the wider audience:*]

Artemisia Gentileschi is indeed telling the truth . . .
—from her own perspective.
She is innocent of any wilful perjury—
—as people may convince themselves of anything
When it benefits their cause.
Signora Gentileschi—I do absolutely pity your situation.
But I must weigh the ledgers carefully.
And with the seriousness of the testimonies presented against you,
And no real rebuttal given except by—
Interested parties such as
Your father and yourself, who stand
Only to benefit from such claims
And since by your own confession you have
Consented to this man again and again and may have come
To regret such submission, once you found out his
Admittedly shameful deception—desperation makes for an unreliable narrator, Signora. Thus, I must unfortunately lean on the side of the defendant and find
Him innocent of said—

MATTEO:
Wait!

[MATTEO *suddenly appears from our audience, the gallery—he is trembling, scared out of his wits.*]

JUDGE:
Who are you?

AGOSTINO:
I don't know this boy, Your Honor.

MATTEO:
I—I—I am Matteo Favale. And there is—
no benefit to me, speaking. At all.
The boys shall all beat me for it.

AGOSTINO:
He is not called before the court!

ARTEMISIA:
Little Matteo, always the weakest and the least promising—

MATTEO:
Signora Gentileschi is speaking the truth, Your Honor.

ARTEMISIA:
And the other boys all teased him—

MATTEO:
I saw it all happen—the first time.
Just as she said.
And just as—terribly as she said.

ARTEMISIA:
For being apprenticed to me.

MATTEO:
I was whipped for dropping the red pigment.

ARTEMISIA:
And though he had more cause, he was the only one—who did not hate me for it.

MATTEO:
I did not want to be whipped worse for—
Seeing what I saw.
I wanted Signora Gentileschi to go on and keep working
So she could teach me how to—become a real artist
If she came to ruin, I would come to ruin.
But she was always kind to me.

[*To Artemisia:*]

I am sorry—that I did not stop it.
Signore.

AGOSTINO:

Are—what, are you going to take the word of this boy—whoever he is—

MATTEO:

Matteo Favale.

AGOSTINO:

Over my own? Over all of the—the testimony you have heard today, over this woman's admitted behavior, over her own consent, over and over and—

JUDGE:

Let it never be said, dear people, that Rome is not a city of rules!

AGOSTINO:

He is not even called before the court!!!

JUDGE:

I find that Agostino Tassi is guilty both of despoiling Artemisia Gentileschi, daughter of Orazio Gentileschi—and the theft of artwork belonging to same Orazio.

AGOSTINO:

Your Honor—

JUDGE:

I order ten lashes in the nearest public square to the servant Tuzia Medaglia for her part in said despoilment—

AGOSTINO:

Your Honor!

JUDGE:

And for Agostino Tassi—three years of imprisonment.
One for the deflowering, two for the painting.
Take him away.

[*The* DEPUTY *begins to lead* AGOSTINO *away; the crowd murmurs.*]

AGOSTINO [*righteously*]:

I am a good man, Your Honor—an innocent man! I have written to my friends in the highest circles—and they will answer! Your Honor! Your Honor, please!!

[*The* DEPUTY *pushes him out—just as* ORAZIO *comes back in—he stares at* ARTEMISIA—*for a moment, all that's heard is the murmur of the crowd.*]

JUDGE:

Signore and Signora Gentileschi—I congratulate you on a rare and precious justice.

[ARTEMISIA *turns to go, then—*]

But—before I dismiss this assembly—you must do your part.

ORAZIO:

My—?

JUDGE:

Signora—I say before all gathered here that because Agostino Tassi is guilty—does not make you free from blame. Even a nun who is violated may not return to a convent after her ruin. And you are no nun.

Your own conduct has led you to this end.

ARTEMISIA:

Your Honor—

JUDGE:

I suggest that you repent—deeply, and with all humility.

ARTEMISIA:

(I—)

JUDGE:

Start Now, Signora.

[*Beat.*]

We will wait.

[ARTEMISIA, *painfully, unable to use her maimed hands, gets to her knees. All assembled watch—church bells begin in the distance, as the scene transitions. She need not get through more than the Latin, if you do not need all the text for the transition.*]

ARTEMISIA:

Miserere mei, Deus: secundum magnam misericordiam tuam. Et secundum multitudinem miserationum tuarum, dele iniquitatem meam.
Make me a clean heart, O God; and cast me not away from Thy presence.
For a broken and contrite spirit, O God, shalt thou not despise.
Miserere mei Deus—For my sin is ever before me!

[*The church bells build, as we transition back to* ORAZIO*'s studio. Days later.* ARTEMISIA *exits.*]

6

[COSIMO *says goodbye to* ORAZIO*—grasping his arms.*]

COSIMO:

Buona notte, Orazio. And may these dark days—soon be just a distant memory.

ORAZIO:

From your lips to God's ears, old friend. Arrivederci.

[*They kiss cheeks and embrace.* ARTEMISIA *enters, just before* COSIMO *leaves. Her hands are painful. She watches him go.* ORAZIO *turns and sees her—*]

ORAZIO:
—Ah. Artemisia.

ARTEMISIA:
Papa. Was that—Cosimo, I just saw leaving?

ORAZIO:
I thought you were lying down—

ARTEMISIA:
What was he—

ORAZIO:
How are your hands? [*Beat.*]
We must get you some salve. I'll see if I have anything, in the back.
[*He begins to leave.*]

ARTEMISIA:
Papa. What—was Cosimo doing here?

ORAZIO:
Making his apologies, my dear. Mending fences.
Cosimo is an honorable man, you know—and in defense of honorable men—[*he clears his throat*] well. He thought he had a duty to say his piece. [*Beat.*]
And he also had some very kind things to say about—he does think my fresco is—coming along.

ARTEMISIA:
The fresco?

ORAZIO:
Of course, it's a tremendous amount of work, now that it's just me. But Cosimo agrees—it has true potential. It might be my greatest accomplishment yet, who knows? A real—phoenix rising out of the flames moment. The people will certainly be paying attention.
Cosimo has even offered—to help me finish one or two of / the—

ARTEMISIA:

/ You're finishing the fresco. So you'll preserve—Agostino's paintings. Your collaboration.

ORAZIO:

Something good can still come out of all this.

ARTEMISIA:

And you'll work with Cosimo again. After what he said.

ORAZIO:

He said he was sorry.

ARTEMISIA:

To *you.*

ORAZIO:

This tribe—is a small tribe, the brotherhood of artists! I cannot afford to keep enemies! I need to succeed, to make a living—and not just for me!

For you. For your future.

Misia—I have—made some arrangements.

ARTEMISIA:

What arrangements?

ORAZIO:

There is a man. Pierantonio Stiattesi. A kind man—a widower. He knows your—situation. And he lives in Florence, so you can—get away from here.

ARTEMISIA:

You don't—you want to—marry me off to some stranger?

ORAZIO:

You will like him!

ARTEMISIA:

—and what if I don't?!!!!

ORAZIO:

We are lucky that he is so understanding, given that you . . . [*Beat.*] —This is—a good match, considering. And even so—even so, with Pierantonio—a compassionate, reasonable fellow, I must give—a considerable dowry!

I had to sell—several paintings.

ARTEMISIA:

Which paintings.

ORAZIO:

The *Susanna*. The *Madonna*.

ARTEMISIA:

My paintings!

ORAZIO:

And others, and others! For your sake!

ARTEMISIA:

And so you sell me off, as well as my art!!!!!!!

ORAZIO:

I cannot have you—in danger, anymore! I cannot have you in the studio!

ARTEMISIA:

No, that would be bad for business!!!!!!

ORAZIO:

Justice has been served! We must find a way to move on!

I have sacrificed, too. I have suffered. I spent thousands to bring the case to court, not to mention the cost to my reputation—

ARTEMISIA:

You gave for you. For YOU. I never asked you to!

Whose justice was served, Papa!

I spoke only the truth, and either they didn't care—or they didn't believe me

And I don't know which is worse.
Only the voice of a ten-year-old boy saved me!
His word was worth more than my own!
The trial was as bad as the rape—worse, worse—because the violation was all done in the name of integrity!
So what fucking wrong was even undone?!
What was ever made aright—except *your* precious fucking honor?!

ORAZIO:
—I tried to protect you. I know that I have failed.
So now I will not fail again. You will be safe with Pierantonio.

ARTEMISIA:
What of—my work here? What of—commissions, and—and joining the guild??

ORAZIO:
They'll never let you join the guild. They never would have.
We all must make compromises. And that is the truth.

ARTEMISIA:
The truth—the truth is that you will never remake the world, Papa.
You can never be a great master.
You don't have the vision for it.

ORAZIO:
I shall write to you in Florence, my dear.

[*He begins to leave.*]

ARTEMISIA [*like a child again*]:
Papa. Please. Please don't send me away.

ORAZIO:
Misia—stop. You know it pains me to deny you.

[ARTEMISIA *looks around her father's studio. The canvases on the wall—the easels. She touches one—and throws it across the room. She tears the studio apart. She rips the canvases off the wall. She sinks down in the ruined studio—puts her head in her hands—a beat. She raises her head. Church bells ring.*]

7

ARTEMISIA:
I meet Pierantonio the next day.
He's an old man, wealthy—and his hand is dry when he takes my own.
That's all I know. And yet
I marry him the day after that.
What else can I do?
Slit my wrists, swallow belladonna?
I want to live.
Should I burn the studio down, with my father in it?
In spite of everything—I still love him.
He gives me away to my new husband at the altar—
But I will not take his blessing.

Three days later, I am in a cart
Rattling off to my new life.
The last thing my father says to me is:

ORAZIO:
Forgive—and forget.

ARTEMISIA:
Papa raises his hand in farewell
Though I close my eyes not to see it.
I ride away from my fallen God, my father
And I think—that is the last time
I'll see divinity upon this earth.

The cart rattles away
And as Rome, that broken city

grows smaller in the distance—
I feel what a fool I have been.
Why did I ever think—that they would welcome me, thank me
For trying to be smarter and stronger—
For wanting to best them at their own game?
Why did I ever believe I could be the exception to the rule?
I, I, I,
am headed to Florence, the hub of all
Art in Italy, full of patrons and masters and inspiration, and I feel—
Nothing.
Why try?
They've ruined me, in every way.
I've lost—
My father, my faith, my art,
Even my story.
And I accept it—that I am no longer
In control of the narrative.
I will run away from the past,
But I can see no future.

8

ARTEMISIA:
Pierantonio Stiattesi is indeed kind
And he does not expect much.
I lie beneath his weight the first night,
I close my eyes,
I think of the spider weaving her web
On my father's ceiling
Hidden away from the world of men
Even from those who claim to love her.
Pierantonio does not seem to realize
That I am frozen beneath him.
Or maybe he does—for after that first night,

He does not trouble me often.
Days go by, then months—
I live in Florence, now, but I do not
Walk upon the streets, or stick my head out of windows.
I know the price of straying too far.
I have finally learned a lady's trade.
I stay chastely within my husband's house,
Sequestered, and protected, and very very still.
And after a time
A child comes—a little girl.

[*A servant hands* ARTEMISIA *a baby—she looks at it, sadly.*]

I am permitted to name her Prudenzia, after my sad-eyed mother—
I do not hold her often.
I entrust her to the wet nurse.

[*She hands the baby back to the servant.*]

I cannot feel my body
And so I feel my child as something apart from myself—
Something belonging to my husband.
I feel as remote to her as my mother, the icon on the wall—
For though I did not die in the childbed . . .

. . . my father said to me: forgive, forget—
And you shall feel safe.

But I, I, I—so often
wake up in the middle
Of the night with terrible weight on my chest,
My throat—trying to speak—
But choked—gasping and shaking, with no voice.
Often I sit up with a candle, burning low, and then another—
And then another, and then another,
Until I can see the morning light over the terra-cotta roofs of the city.
I've grown afraid of the dark.

My husband is not blind to this—peculiarity
And he would rather I not waste the tallow.
He suggests, vaguely, that perhaps I should start painting again.
As a harmless little hobby.
Indeed, he sets up a small room
At the front of the house
A sort of studio.
He even has the canvas stretched for me—
Why should I do it myself, he says
I am a lady now.

9

[ARTEMISIA's *makeshift studio.*]

ARTEMISIA:
And so every day
I go and I sit in my makeshift studio.
And watch the shadows play upon the walls.

[*She lays the baby down in a crib.*]

Sometimes I bring the baby, place her in her crib as she sleeps.

[*She stands in front of a blank canvas, surveying it—and flexes her hands.*]

This room—is one of my own.
I am free, to—to do whatever I like,
To create whatever picture I prefer.
But—I never make a mark.
Not once.

What had once been
Easy and effortless, flowing through me like sunlight
From above

Now I cannot—
Find the silence.
My thoughts are much too loud.
I have no confidence in any action—
I do not know where to put my hands.

I, I, I—
I stare at the blank canvas.
Blankness stares back.
I do not feel the divine spark I once did,
Only blank—
Day after day, nothing for nothing, and nothing as far
As my future can—

MARIA:
Signora Gentileschi.

10

[MARIA *has suddenly appeared in the studio.* ARTEMISIA *stares at her—she cannot place her, at first.* MARIA *is clothed in a dust-covered traveling hood.*]

MARIA:
Buongiorno, Signora Gentileschi. It's me.
Don't you remember—

ARTEMISIA:
Madre di Dio.

MARIA:
—Maria.

ARTEMISIA:
Yes, I—I know. Maria.
—What are / you doing—

MARIA:

/ Do you mind if I come in?

[MARIA *walks in, not waiting for an answer.*]

ARTEMISIA [*yes*]:

Why—no.

MARIA:

The studio is a bit of an upgrade from the one in Rome, huh? Cleaner, at least.

ARTEMISIA:

—it has never been used.

MARIA:

Is it yours?

ARTEMISIA:

—I suppose so, yes, although really, it—it belongs to my husband.

MARIA:

No. I mean. [*She gestures to the baby in the cradle.*]

ARTEMISIA:

Oh. Yes.

MARIA:

Girl or boy?

ARTEMISIA:

Girl.

MARIA:

Poor thing.

ARTEMISIA:

Maria—

MARIA:

Do you have any water?
My throat is dry, I was on the road all yesterday—and that dust, it digs down into your bones.

[ARTEMISIA *pours her a cup of water from a jug. As she does:*]

ARTEMISIA:

You—you have just arrived in Florence?

MARIA:

Rome was getting small. The company—tiresome. And I can work—anywhere.

ARTEMISIA:

As a model?

MARIA:

That, too.

[ARTEMISIA *hands her the water.*]

ARTEMISIA:

Maria, may I ask—why you are—here?

MARIA:

They say Florence is a big art town, yes?

ARTEMISIA:

Bigger than Rome, even.

MARIA:

Then I've come to the right place.
—And so?

ARTEMISIA:

And so, what?

MARIA:

So. Do I have the job.

Don't break my heart, now, Signora Gentileschi. Don't tell me I came all the way on that dusty fucking road for nothing.

ARTEMISIA:

I'm not—you came here—following me?

MARIA:

I liked the way you paint me. Strong. Real. Center. Not like the boys do.

ARTEMISIA:

I'm—I'm afraid—I have no work to offer. I'm not painting, anymore.

MARIA:

But—you have this whole setup here.

ARTEMISIA:

The—the impulse has left me—I am different, now.

[*Beat.*]

MARIA:

Your hands?

ARTEMISIA:

No. [*She hides her hands.*] They're—they've healed.

MARIA:

I heard, you know. What they did to you.

ARTEMISIA:

Everybody heard.

MARIA:

And I saw—that they let Tassi out.

ARTEMISIA:
So my husband told me. Tassi and his connections.

MARIA:
Didn't even serve a fucking year, huh? [*She spits.*] Bastards.

[*Beat.*]

ARTEMISIA:
Wait—what do you mean, you—you "saw"?

MARIA:
I spotted him. Several times. He was hanging around the studios again, drinking at the artists' bars, fraternizing with the same old guild boys.

ARTEMISIA:
These were—he was with my father's friends? He was—was he ever with my——

[*Beat. beat beat beat.*]

MARIA:
You didn't know, eh? You must not often hear from your dear Papa.

ARTEMISIA:
—He writes letters.
But I can't read.
And I tell my husband not to even open them.

MARIA:
You see why I wanted to leave Rome.

ARTEMISIA:
I am—very sorry you've come all this way, Signora. But I'm not working, anymore.

MARIA:
Agostino Tassi is working.

ARTEMISIA:
What?

MARIA:
He's being commissioned again.

ARTEMISIA [*barely able to speak*]:
What?!!!!!

MARIA:
Patrons love a scandal. But you've quit?

ARTEMISIA:
And that's—that's why. That's fucking why!

MARIA:
You don't have the inspiration?

ARTEMISIA:
Why should I? Why should I?! For those men, for this—sick system of winks and back-slapping and brotherhood and patrons—I've suffered enough! I was ruined, lost my honor—for—for nothing!!

MARIA:
He lost his honor. Not you.

ARTEMISIA:
Funny—that's not what they say.
You should go.

MARIA:
I haven't finished my water.

[*She takes a big swallow, then—*]

You know—you are not the only female artist I ever met.

I had an older sister once—who liked to scratch pictures in the clay with sticks,
The sun would dry them out, and they'd last awhile.
She'd draw me anything I asked for—
Dogs, cats, the face of our mother.
And I thought they were—amazing.
Now, it was a long time ago, and—I was very young.
Maybe she wasn't so great. Maybe not a master, who knows?
but to me it was magic—
She made something out of nothing.
To me, she was a Goddess.

ARTEMISIA:
Please, you need to—

MARIA:
But of course, nobody was going to pay for drawings made in the dirt.
She entered this profession—not the modeling—but the other—
Same as I did.
But she started even younger.
We needed the money.
And some fucking client—picked her of all the other working girls one night—
And within the year, a pox carried her away.
Without me, nobody would remember her.
Certainly not her drawings.
Nobody remembers her story.

ARTEMISIA:
I'm sorry about your—

MARIA:
I'm not done.
She never got to learn!
So I'll never know if she was really any good.
We never knew our father,

But whomever he was, he was not a painter to teach us.
We didn't have that luxury. Not like you.

ARTEMISIA:
Luxury! I had to fight—every day, to /

MARIA:
/ And you won some, didn't you?!
You actually won some, and now you want to give up?

ARTEMISIA:
I don't have the heart to do it anymore!

MARIA:
—I am sorry about what happened to you. I am. [ARTEMISIA *scoffs, is about to retort.*]
But do you think you're the only one?
I told you, you should have asked me!
You think the men listened to a no from me, if they didn't from you?
You think those boys in the studio didn't do things—you think Tassi only
Went after you?
Justice doesn't exist for women like me!
The most I could expect was commerce—
At least your father paid for it!

ARTEMISIA:
. . . . . . my father?

MARIA:
Of course.
—I wager it must eat away at your soul
Working amongst men like that
Trying to be like them, impress them, get in their circles.
Making your work for their eyes,
And having them hate you for it.
SO MOTHERFUCKING. STOP. IT.

ARTEMISIA:
What?

MARIA:
I know you thought you were the only woman,
Maybe even *liked* being the only woman in those rooms—
But you weren't! You never were!
IT'S NOT ONLY YOUR STORY.
AND YOU DON'T GET TO LET THEM BE THE ONLY TELLER.
YOU'RE GOING TO LET THEM—ALL OF THEM, COSIMO, TASSI, YOUR FATHER, FUCKING BEAT YOU?!
NO. YOU DON'T STOP FIGHTING.
GET LOUDER. GET BOLDER.
YOU BE SO BIG THEY CAN'T BLOCK YOU OUT.
YOU TELL THE FUCKING TRUTH.
AND YOU MAKE THEM FUCKING CHOKE ON IT.
You have the opportunity, and so many didn't!
And so you don't forgive! You don't forget!
You don't get to give up!
Because you DON'T DO IT FOR THEM, you understand?!!
You do it for fucking us.
Not just you—not just one woman, Artemisia Gentileschi—us.
Now pick up the fucking brush. And paint.

[MARIA *sits, with force, frustrated.*]

I came all the way—to fucking—Florence.

[*Beat.*]

ARTEMISIA [*half to herself*]:
C- . . .
Composition, that's where you begin.

MARIA:
Well?

ARTEMISIA:
I—I want you to pose—as if—you are holding a knife.
To kill a man.

[*Maria grins with relish.*]

11

[MARIA *begins to pose, à la* Judith Beheading Holofernes—*the strong downward stroke—as* ARTEMISIA *picks up her brush, and*—]

ARTEMISIA:
For the first time, I pick up my brush in my scarred hands
And I feel that divine spark again
But different—
Not God, but—a Goddess
I built divinity in the shape of my father—
But it was not him but her
Her all along—
For the first time, since—
I can feel my body again!
My body, which
Kept me alive through all these trials—
How could I blame it for their sins!

I am not channeling just one spirit now—
And my fear begins to lift away—
And the first thing I paint—
Is what opened my eyes all those years ago!

[*Behind her flashes Artemisia's* Judith Beheading Holofernes.]

Artemisia Gentileschi, *Judith Beheading Holofernes,* ca. 1620.
Oil on canvas. Galleria degli Uffizi, Florence.
Photography: Gabinetto Fotografico delle Gallerie degli Uffizi.

Judith beheading Holofernes!
But I do not paint it like even the great Caravaggio
I do not want to follow a master anymore—
I do not paint it as slender Judith
Wincing ladylike, away!
This Judith is weighty, her arms are flexed,
Her body is strong enough to do the act—
But not alone!
Never again alone!
Not I but she—not she but we—
His hand clamps on a throat but she
Presses on—and together we hold the beast down—
And strike hard enough to kill—!

It is this—it is her—and her—and her—and her—
That changes everything for me.

[*Painting after painting of the dozens done by Artemisia Gentileschi begin to appear behind her—over and over, the masterpieces, dozens of them.*]

ARTEMISIA:
I find that I can work again!
I paint, and I paint, and I paint.
Always women, always center—
And I don't just paint ladies and saints
I paint whores and nurses and servants!
I paint them strong, I paint them angry!
My women never weep!
And my prostitutes look like Madonnas and vice versa—
And no one is the ideal!

Scandal is profitable, my papa always said—
And out from under his shadow—
My paintings finally begin to sell.

I am never accepted to their brotherhood—
But I do not need to be!
Over the next few decades,
I paint masterpiece upon masterpiece—
For the gentry, for the bishops—
For courts all over Europe—
I travel abroad, run my own business—
I learn to read and to write!
And when my husband leaves me
Because my hobby has become my life
I take a lover and I learn how my body may make
Its own pleasure, its own provenance—
I bear my children, and I do not make them my familiars—
And I never will send them away!

I sit amongst masters!
I make friends with Vouet, Medicis, Galileo!
I charge thrice as much as any man and they pay it gladly!
The impulse came *back*—not the same
But from above *and*
Below! From the earth herself
I felt my silent mother's bones,
The mother who named me something scandalous all those years ago—
Goading me on.

My work sells, and sells, and eventually hangs
Next to Michelangelo, Donatello—
Even Caravaggio, my first love—
It hangs in the homes of kings and queens!
Even in the halls of the papacy—
My women snarl from the canvas!

[*Particular paintings appear, all projected behind her—the many, many times Artemisia Gentileschi painted Susanna and the Elders and Judith and her maidservant—all sharing the screen together.*]

And there are two themes I come to again and again
Susanna, defiant in her garden
And Judith and her compatriot,
Strong enough to wield the knife together.
I paint them over and over—
I cannot stop—the surprise, the violation—
The action, the revenge—
The women act to save their people—
They will not forgive! They do not forget.

Dozens, and dozens, and dozens,
Carved from darkness into life!
I work until my death!
I take my last breath,
Turning toward the picture
She has made in my
Mind!
And when people have forgotten my poor father's work
My God, my Judas
Caught by the traditions of his time
They still remember me!
And not just me!
Us!
Me and her together!
Captured and free forever
We struggle to hold the tyrant down!

With every painting I said a prayer—
Every daughter of mothers who ever sees this work
Will know she is not alone
She will see what it means
To fight, despite the hands at your throat.
To use your holy anger—
To carve the light across the dark

[*All the pictures of Artemisia Gentileschi flash faster and faster across the screen, now all of them projected across* MARIA'*s body.*]

Not for them, for us—
Not my story but ours,
And not their narrative to tell!
We will try, in our brief time, to remake the world—
Not just for us, but for the ones to come—
For all the stories that are yet untold.

[ARTEMISIA *steps into the projection also—and as the paintings flash across her body as well.*]

I hope you hear me—do you hear me—
Must we tell it again—
Fighting across the ages—
That it is
Not I, I, I,
but we, we, we here—
And we are never alone!

[ARTEMISIA *and* MARIA *look toward the audience—surrounded by images of the women—and above them all* Judith Beheading Holofernes—*fighting on and on.*]